# Praise

"The greatest value in this book lies in the insights of how to become an effective leader. Barrows and Downing share skill-building techniques that ensure success throughout your career."
— **Ted Fleming**, former Head of Talent Development, CVS Health, and author of *Develop*

"Do you want to become a sharper leader? Authors Ed Barrows and Laura M Downing give you the comprehensive volume of essential leader abilities that cover all the bases you'll need for yourself and the people around you. Take this self-directed master class for your next promotion."
— **Randy White**, Founding Partner, The Executive Development Group, LLC and Co-author, *Relax, It's Only Uncertainty and Breaking the Glass Ceiling*

"It's essential in our nonprofit sector to develop and manage aspiring leaders. In this dynamic environment, *Twelve Skills* is a go-to guide for success."
— **Michael D Weekes**, President/CEO- Providers' Council in Massachusetts and former board chair of the National Council of Nonprofits

"Like a Swiss army knife, this book provides exactly what you need to lead with success. From strategic thinking to solving the right problems, Barrows and Downing zoom in on the few key ideas that really matter, providing powerful hands-on advice and ample real-world examples to go with it. Tackle one skill per week, or go straight to your most pressing issue; either way, this book will quickly make you a better leader."

— **Thomas Wedell-Wedellsborg,** bestselling author of *What's Your Problem?* (Harvard Business Review Press)

"Whether you want to build your skills by zooming in on particular leadership battles or zooming out on the overall leadership battlefield, Twelve Skills provides you an actionable map of the terrain. Putting Barrows and Downing's frameworks and recommendations into practice will make you a more effective leader."

— **Bruce Roberson**, Partner, Brightstar Capital Partners and Co-Author *What Really Works*

# Twelve Skills

The guide to becoming a stronger leader and accelerating your career

Ed Barrows & Laura M. Downing

# R<sup>e</sup>think

First published in Great Britain in 2023 by Rethink Press (www.rethinkpress.com)

© Copyright Ed Barrows and Laura M. Downing

All rights reserved. No part of this publication may be reproduced, stored in or introduced into a retrieval system, or transmitted, in any form, or by any means (electronic, mechanical, photocopying, recording or otherwise) without the prior written permission of the publisher.

The right of Ed Barrows and Laura M. Downing to be identified as the authors of this work has been asserted by them in accordance with the Copyright, Designs and Patents Act 1988.

This book is sold subject to the condition that it shall not, by way of trade or otherwise, be lent, resold, hired out, or otherwise circulated without the publisher's prior consent in any form of binding or cover other than that in which it is published and without a similar condition including this condition being imposed on the subsequent purchaser.

Cover image © Adobe Stock | Vlad Ra27

*To every person who believes there is a leader within*

## With gratitude from Ed Barrows

*To my six kids—Henry, Hannah, Ava, Hugh, Howard, and Ingrid—who remind me every day the importance of being a good role model*

*To my wonderful wife Nadine, who epitomizes leadership by example*

## With gratitude from Laura M Downing

*To my parents, who taught me how to love well and work hard*

*To David P Norton, who shows me how to lead, learn, and grow, all the time*

*To my husband, Gerald, and our son, Isaac, who bring me joy and inspiration every day*

# Contents

**Introduction**    1
    Why Twelve Skills?    1
    Who we are    2
    Why we wrote this book    4
    Why you should read this book now    6
    How to use this book    7
    Leadership skills can be learned    10
    Chapter guide    11

**1 Mastering Strategic Thinking**    19
    Why strategic thinking?    20
    Chapter goals    21
    Strategic thinking defined    23
    Skill builder One: GAPS strategic thinking process    24
    Getting started with strategic thinking    45

| | | |
|---|---|---|
| **2** | **Unlocking Problem Solving** | **47** |
| | Why problem solving? | 48 |
| | Chapter goals | 50 |
| | Problem solving defined | 52 |
| | Skill builder Two: D2A2 problem-solving process | 52 |
| | Getting started with problem solving | 67 |
| **3** | **Enhancing Executive Presence** | **71** |
| | Why executive presence? | 72 |
| | Chapter goals | 75 |
| | Executive presence defined | 76 |
| | Skill builder Three: ABC executive presence process | 77 |
| | Getting started with executive presence | 91 |
| **4** | **Developing Clear Messaging** | **93** |
| | Why clear messaging? | 94 |
| | Chapter goals | 96 |
| | Clear messaging defined | 98 |
| | Skill builder Four: 5C clear messaging process | 99 |
| | Getting started with effective messaging | 115 |
| **5** | **Expanding Relationship Building** | **117** |
| | Why relationship building? | 118 |
| | Chapter goals | 118 |

| | | |
|---|---|---|
| | Relationship building defined | 120 |
| | Skill builder Five: 3E relationship-building process | 121 |
| | Getting started with relationship building | 136 |
| **6** | **Strengthening Talent Development** | **139** |
| | Why talent development? | 140 |
| | Chapter goals | 140 |
| | Talent development defined | 142 |
| | Skill builder Six: HDCM talent development process | 143 |
| | Getting started with talent development | 163 |
| **7** | **Invigorating Team Building** | **165** |
| | Why team building? | 166 |
| | Chapter goals | 167 |
| | Team defined | 168 |
| | Elements of a real team | 169 |
| | Skill builder Seven: 3D team-building process | 170 |
| | Getting started with team building | 190 |
| **8** | **Improving Group Collaboration** | **193** |
| | Why collaboration? | 194 |
| | Chapter goals | 195 |

| | |
|---|---|
| Collaboration definition | 197 |
| What effective collaboration looks like | 198 |
| When to collaborate (and when not to) | 200 |
| Skill builder Eight: 3P collaboration process | 201 |
| Getting started with effective collaboration | 219 |

**9 Revamping Change Leadership** — **221**

| | |
|---|---|
| Why change leadership? | 222 |
| Chapter goals | 223 |
| Change leadership defined | 224 |
| Skill builder Nine: PTS change leadership process | 226 |
| Getting started with change management | 245 |

**10 Increasing Persuasion and Influence** — **247**

| | |
|---|---|
| Why persuasion and influence? | 248 |
| Chapter goals | 249 |
| Skill builder Ten: Our 3P framework | 251 |
| Getting started with persuasion and influence | 269 |

**11 Driving Focused Execution** — **271**

| | |
|---|---|
| Why execution? | 272 |
| Chapter goals | 273 |
| Execution defined | 274 |

| | |
|---|---|
| Skill builder Eleven: The 4M execution process | 275 |
| Getting started with focused execution | 295 |

**12 Achieving Top-Tier Performance** — **297**

| | |
|---|---|
| Why top-tier performance? | 298 |
| Chapter goals | 300 |
| What we know about top-performing organizations | 301 |
| Top-tier performance defined | 304 |
| Skill builder Twelve: Four primary practices | 304 |
| Secondary practices | 305 |
| Putting it all together | 326 |
| Getting started with top-tier performance | 328 |

| | |
|---|---|
| **Conclusion** | **329** |
| Where to go next | 329 |
| Your action guide for stronger leadership | 330 |
| One step that rules them all | 331 |
| **Notes** | **333** |
| **Acknowledgments** | **345** |
| **The Authors** | **347** |

# Introduction

## Why Twelve Skills?

If you've picked up this book, you're either already a rising leader or wanting to become one. Maybe you have been selected to lead a team for the first time and aren't sure where to start. You're possibly a manager or director looking to sharpen your leadership skills on your way to the next level. It could be you're someone who has missed out on promotions and has got to the point where you want to do something about it. Regardless of the reason, you've come to the right place.

Being an aspiring leader can be lonely and even frustrating. You may be technically proficient and have ridden these skills right into a leadership role. Now, however, your technical skills won't help you as much as they used to—in fact, they may even hamper your performance. Doubling down on what, in the past, were seen as strengths might set you back performance-wise. Now you've realized you need a new, complete set of skills—skills that will help you set direction, build your team, create allies, influence your peers, and deliver results. What you need are our Twelve Skills.

We've created *Twelve Skills: The guide to becoming a stronger leader and accelerating your career* to help managers at all levels not just succeed but also excel. If you're happy working as an individual contributor or subject-matter expert and don't aspire to be a people leader, you will still need many of these Twelve Skills to be effective in your role. On the other hand, if you're someone with the desire to get ahead—someone who knows you're capable of taking on more responsibility—this book is also for you. It's a lean but power-packed guide on the skills you need to set yourself apart in any role.

## Who we are

Why learn leadership from us? Because our knowledge of this topic is both deep and diverse. Together we have more than sixty years in consulting, education, and coaching. We've had the opportunity to work with leaders in virtually every sector—large for-profit companies, startups, military organizations, government agencies, and nonprofit organizations.

## INTRODUCTION

We've worked with individual leaders and leadership teams at all management levels—senior, mid-career, and rising leaders—in a broad range of industries.

Our early focus was strategy consulting. For years we worked closely with thought leaders who created the field of strategy. Our work taught us that it's not just strategy that matters but also teamwork, communication, and measurement. We found that execution follows great leadership. There is a major difference in results when a leader models, empowers, and inspires others to confront challenges, celebrate learning, and leverage teamwork, and focuses everyone's attention on delivering high performance. In fact, many of our clients have won awards for excellence in delivering results.

We're also experienced educators who've taught in traditional academic settings, ranging from Babson and Boston Colleges to Northeastern, Simmons and Harvard Universities. We've created and delivered professional development programs for nonprofits, government agencies, and large corporations, much of it with Duke Corporate Education—a global leader in executive development. We discovered that there are many ways for people to learn, and the more modes you call on to engage people while learning, the better. Further, the more hands-on and experiential your learning is, the more likely it is to stick.

Lastly, we're ICF-certified coaches who've worked with middle managers and CEOs through CLIR

Coaching, a coaching organization focused on accountability-based coaching. Here we've seen that people are most committed to their own professional development when they have a voice in it. Their commitment and attention will be far greater than if they're compelled to attend a day-long seminar or take a mandatory online class.

To ensure our views aren't based purely on our own experience, we have filtered what we've discovered through a review of leadership literature and programs published by the top organizations that research and teach on the topic. These include Harvard Business Publishing, McKinsey Quarterly, Franklin Covey, Zenger & Folkman, Heidrick & Struggles, Development Dimensions International, *Psychology Today*, and more.

Boiling down all that research, we have learned that even if a manager is a brilliant visionary or highly creative thinker, a defined set of essential leadership skills is still required to deliver results. The skills needed for leadership excellence are consistent across all organization sizes and types. Ask any expert in any sector about leadership, and the same Twelve Skills come up over and over again. These are the skills outlined in this book.

## Why we wrote this book

There are three reasons for us bringing you this book and its twelve core leadership skills.

## INTRODUCTION

First, capable leadership is needed now more than ever before. In today's flat organizations, leaders are needed at every level. The days of rigid hierarchy, where everyone reports to a supervisor, are gone. Leaders must be able to manage one team or multiple teams. For example, you could be the world's best accountant, but sooner or later, you'll also find yourself managing a team of accountants. Nothing you learn in an accounting program prepares you for that, and this book will fill the gap. Advance into leadership without these skills at your peril.

Second, we work with leaders in a variety of organizations, and these are the very skills that are being taught. If you have an MBA, you've probably learned some of these. If you're part of a HiPo (high potential) group, you've likely already been taught these skills because organizations invest in them. Take our word for it—we're the ones that design and deliver the training. If you don't have an MBA or haven't been fortunate enough to be dubbed high potential, you still deserve the chance to build the skills that set you apart, no matter your current role.

Finally, to truly achieve career success over the long term, leaders need to master a proven set of skills as early as possible in their professional journey. These twelve are the foundational, must-have skills for moving up. The most significant contribution we can make to leader development (and to you) is give you *all* the skills you need to ascend into leadership in an easy-to-read, ready-to-implement format.

## Why you should read this book now

You might be thinking, *Sure, leadership fundamentals—how can that matter in today's fast-changing world?* We'll answer that question.

The leadership skills we teach in this book aren't the latest fad or some set of special techniques for leading during a trying time. They also won't be outdated a year from now. Think of them like blue jeans and apple pie—things that have stood the test of time and will continue to do so. These are leadership fundamentals for the ages, time-tested through recession, war, and political upheavals of all kinds. As you'll see, we've updated some of the approaches in relation to recent events, but they're still as foundational and applicable as they've ever been.

While we have learned from all the companies and publications listed above, we have drawn content almost exclusively from Harvard Business Publishing (HBP)—the world leader on topics ranging from strategy to leadership. We have deep ties to Harvard, both being instructors in Harvard's Division of Continuing Education, and Laura being a Harvard Business School graduate. Both of us have also published articles with HBP. You can be assured that the thoughts and ideas in this book are drawn from the best source of management thinking today and have been tested both in the classroom and online at Harvard, as well as in the real world.

Despite the wide-ranging availability of trusted sources, many leaders still don't possess core skills. While managers often advance in their careers with well developed technical skill sets, eventually they hit a wall. That wall will stop progress in its track and hold those managers back from greater levels of success. No matter which way technology evolves or what geopolitical changes occur, you need to master the Twelve Skills covered in this book. Otherwise, your career will be stymied.

This book will immediately pay you dividends. It's based on simple steps and proven activities that work. Even if you don't master all twelve, moving the dial on just a few will start to make your colleagues recognize that you are a higher-caliber leader.

The face of the workplace continues to evolve. Mounting volumes of work, distributed over a larger network and across more teams, means we now have less time to commit to formal leadership education. The same is happening in corporations, nonprofit organizations, and governments. They're simply not investing broadly in their people the way they used to, which means that those who want to get ahead have to make the effort on their own.

## How to use this book

Many books are written in a linear way, where you're meant to read the chapters in order.

**TWELVE SKILLS**

This book can be read that way too, but it can also be started from any chapter. Each of the Twelve Skills stands on its own as an important ingredient for leadership success. If acquiring one skill is an urgent priority in your career right now, feel free to begin your leadership learning with that chapter.

The book has six primary topics, with two chapters illuminating the facets—the two skills—of each leadership area. As you can see in this graphic, these topics together form a complete circle of leadership mastery.

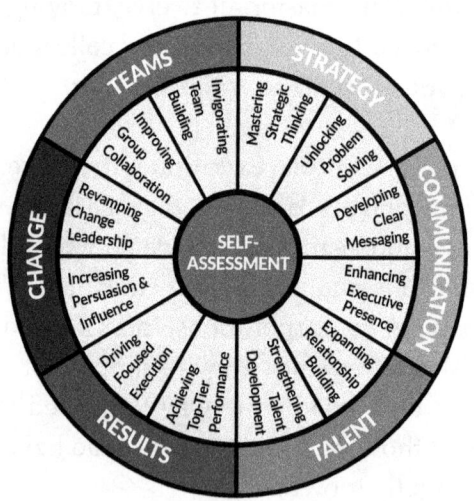

*The Twelve Skills*

Each chapter can lead logically on to the next. Alternatively, you can opt to learn a specific topic, followed by a set of complementary skills that lie directly across from that topic on the dartboard.

## INTRODUCTION

After you have learned to think strategically, you might want to discover how to use strategy to achieve top-tier performance. Once you've learned to develop talent, you might want to next delve into how to manage teams of people. If you've just sharpened your messaging abilities, you might choose to learn how to use communication to persuade and influence more effectively.

You might otherwise have recognized specific areas you need to develop, which lie at random points in the dartboard. It's a modular framework that allows you to follow your interests and learn according to your own priorities.

You will also notice that self-assessment lies at the core of all of the Twelve Skills. Each chapter begins with a self-assessment for that particular skill set. The overall comprehensive assessment is located at www.surveymonkey.com/r/TwelveSkills2. We suggest that readers take the assessment when beginning to read the book and again at the end after you have tried to make improvements to your chosen skills. We would also like to invite you to join our LinkedIn community. There you can engage with other Twelve Skills leaders and access new content.

We've designed this book so we can teach it to management students as a course, in person, or online. You can also use it as the basis for an individual, independent-study leadership-skills curriculum, for yourself or for your whole team.

We'd like to make one important note at this point about reading leadership books: Reading a book won't make you a great leader. As packed with practical strategies as our book is, reading it won't magically transform you into a leadership genius. You have to complete one more step to become a dynamic leader: In the end, you have to *take action*.

Make sure you try out the techniques you learn in this book, and then get feedback from the people around you. The people you lead will be your best teachers. We can't tell, for example, if you're a fantastic presenter or if your memos are insensitive, but the people around you can. Consider them as your stakeholders, and ask for their feedback. This is how you get measurable results—ask for feedback, thank those people for it, respond to it, and learn from it.

If you'd like to know how you're faring in each of the skill areas before you start, feel free to take our complementary Twelve Skills Self-Assessment at www.surveymonkey.com/r/TwelveSkills2. With your results in hand, you'll have a good sense of where to start your Twelve Skills improvement journey.

## Leadership skills can be learned

It may seem obvious, but we want to state this point clearly: You *can* learn these skills.

INTRODUCTION

When we hear someone say of a successful executive, "She's a born leader," we cringe a bit inside. Leadership isn't an inborn aptitude only some people can possess. You can build your abilities in each of these areas and achieve mastery if you're willing to learn what works, put it into practice, and adapt it to your own unique work environment.

The dirty secret of organizational work today is that there are many vice presidents who are failing at some of these skills. As you read through this book, you may think of senior officers in your company who are truly inept in some areas—sometimes so poor at vital leadership skills that their jobs are at risk. That spells opportunity for you, as someone who is focused on building your leadership abilities.

This book serves as a step-by-step roadmap to acquiring these critical leadership skills. We promise you that mastering them will advance your career.

## Chapter guide

### Chapter 1: Mastering Strategic Thinking

Of course, this isn't just about thinking—it's about changing what you do in your job. Let's also be clear what it's not about: We aren't telling you to rewrite your enterprise strategy.

Using the tools we describe in this chapter, you will be able to:

- Explain what your company does and where it's headed, in concise layperson's language
- Ask a few incisive questions about potential threats or opportunities and discuss them
- Make a specific recommendation about how to do something differently
- Prioritize your activities to maximize your impact on reaching current goals

## Chapter 2: Unlocking Problem Solving

In this chapter we're going to help you not only define but also solve any business problem, with a simple, step-by-step process that you can apply anytime, anywhere. It will help you think about your challenges in a structured way and work toward solutions in a systematic manner. Using this process will keep you from wasting resources on actions and initiatives that don't solve your real problem.

By the end of this chapter, you will be able to:

- Examine in new and novel ways the problems you and your team face
- Apply critical thinking to poorly defined issues

- Use a structured process to increase the odds you'll reach a favorable solution
- Strengthen your ability to help colleagues solve their challenges

## Chapter 3: Enhancing Executive Presence

As the typical executive leader has evolved and diversified, executive presence has also been transformed. It's time to create your own powerful leadership brand.

This chapter will show you how to:

- Shape your personal style and appearance to both fit in and stand out at work
- Gain awareness of the behaviors that diminish your personal image
- Start projecting greater confidence when interacting with your colleagues
- Make a plan that continues to enhance your personal brand

## Chapter 4: Developing Clear Messaging

Communication is an essential leadership skill—one that many leaders don't do well. That's in part because we need to keep a lot in mind whenever we're communicating.

Where you're done here, you will be able to:

- Gain awareness of how effectively you currently communicate
- Evaluate and incorporate the needs and differences of your audience
- Simplify and structure your communications for maximum impact
- Craft robust messages that reach and resonate with your intended audience

## Chapter 5: Expanding Relationship Building

You've likely been building relationships your whole life. After this chapter, when you interact with others, you'll be more aware of everyone's emotions, including your own. You will also have a sense of what you need to do to grow and harvest value from your network.

When you're done reading this chapter, you will be able to:

- Understand what emotional intelligence (EI) is and how it impacts relationship building
- Learn techniques, start new relationships, and expand and strengthen existing ones
- Discover ways to build and manage your professional network

## Chapter 6: Strengthening Talent Development

By the end of this chapter, you will have a better handle on how to hire and develop talent. Keep in mind: Your team members will be key drivers of your success as a leader, so you want them to be top-tier players.

When you've finished this chapter, you will be able to:

- Attract the talent you need for key positions
- Provide constructive feedback and coaching to employees on their development journeys
- Continually manage performance, using a straightforward process

## Chapter 7: Invigorating Team Building

In this chapter we'll outline the basics of teams: What they are, how they work, and where they go wrong. We'll also give you a process for launching and developing a team.

Using the tools we provide, you will be able to:

- Describe and design the successful configuration of a team
- Launch and develop a team, using a structured process

- Perform the basic responsibilities of a team leader
- Spot the common dysfunctions of a team and plan to mitigate them

## Chapter 8: Improving Group Collaboration

The marketplace has changed, requiring ever-increasing levels of collaboration. The collaborations you work on will also continue to grow in complexity.

The tools we introduce in this chapter will help you:

- Recognize when you need to collaborate (and when you don't)
- Assemble a group of people that will collaborate effectively
- Guide your project successfully and manage conflict
- Make collective progress toward defined goals

## Chapter 9: Revamping Change Leadership

Change is no longer the exception—it is a constant in the workplace. However, attempting it too quickly, or without considering the direct or collateral effects, often leads to failure. Following a structured process can make the crucial difference to any change effort, large or small.

Using the tools we describe in this chapter, you will be able to:

- Prepare yourself and your team for change
- Implement change initiatives more effectively
- Sustain focus on the change

## Chapter 10: Increasing Persuasion and Influence

The principles of persuasion and influence come into play in all aspects of life. Many of us overlook that the fundamentals of these concepts are in fact a science. They can be learned and should be practiced, and you need to develop this skill.

This chapter will increase your knowledge and inspire you to practice so you will be able to:

- Understand and navigate politics in your organization
- Persuade others to listen to your ideas
- Use the principles of influence to get others to act

## Chapter 11: Driving Focused Execution

Strategy execution is not for the faint of heart. It requires teamwork, discipline, and transparency. You will often need to confront difficult tradeoffs, but achieving results is the point, so it is time to learn.

Using the tools we describe in this chapter, you will be able to:

- Map out your objectives for execution in a performance model
- Manage (and eliminate) projects, to align with strategic goals
- Measure progress in execution
- Make decisions more rapidly and effectively

## Chapter 12: Achieving Top-Tier Performance

In this chapter we bring together many of the other concepts discussed in this book. The primary job of a great leader is to drive great performance. You need to provide the focus, transparency, prioritization, and shared commitment to results.

By the end of this chapter, you will be able to:

- Recognize and build top performance in your organization
- Focus your strategy and communicate it clearly
- Execute the most important activities flawlessly
- Foster a performance-oriented culture and organization structure

# 1
# Mastering Strategic Thinking

Imagine this. For the bulk of your career, you've worked for a company that owns and runs hundreds of gas stations in the largest region of the country. Since its founding in the early 1900s, the company has been successful. Revenue and profit have grown steadily as it has bought and built more locations, replicating its winning formula of keeping costs low and stations clean. Recently, though, you've heard reports about the growing production of electric vehicles and how they will eventually comprise the bulk of the automobiles manufactured. You mention this to your boss, and he says, "Electric vehicles taking over gas-powered engines? That's funny. I promise you this—if it even happens, it won't be in our lifetimes."

Fast-forward to the annual all-employee meeting. Top executives announce an aggressive acquisition plan, which will almost double your company's footprint over the next several years. At the end of the presentation, you look around at your fellow employees applauding the bold strategy laid out by senior leaders, and you remember the conversation with your boss. You wonder why no one has even mentioned electric vehicles at the current meeting, but then again, your boss assured you there was nothing to worry about, so you dismiss your concerns once again.

Think a scenario like this is unrealistic? Think again. Companies such as Borders, Blackberry, and Blockbuster all faced similar challenges. Each failed to accurately assess the impact new developments would have on their business, and ultimately, they all failed.

## Why strategic thinking?

Industries and businesses are evolving at an alarming rate. Technology improvements, fueled by digital disruption, are driving changes across a wide swath of industries, from manufacturing to healthcare and transportation to professional services. The implication for top managers is clear: Thinking about the future is something that requires the efforts of the entire organization. The power of all employees is needed to identify and prepare for changes happening now as well as those that will occur in the future.

That means managers can no longer survive—let alone thrive—in their jobs by keeping their heads down and working hard. As one senior leader at a Fortune 10 organization recently told us, "We need managers that can think strategically and there just aren't enough of them around here." This underscores what we've seen ourselves. Most managers are good operators—they keep the lights on, the products flowing, and complete assignments on time. There's nothing wrong with that, but that's table stakes today, not a differentiator. Rare is the strategic thinker—the manager who lifts their eyes from their daily to-do list to see how their world is evolving. If you want to get ahead, you need to think strategically. Those who possess this skill are in high demand.

## Chapter goals

Of course, this isn't just about thinking—it's about changing what you do in your job. Let's also be clear what it's not about: We aren't telling you to rewrite your enterprise strategy.

Using the tools we describe in this chapter, you will be able to:

- Explain what your company does and where it's headed, in concise layperson's language
- Ask a few incisive questions about potential threats or opportunities and discuss them

- Make a specific recommendation about how to do something differently
- Prioritize your activities to maximize your impact on reaching current goals

---

**EXERCISE: Strategic thinking—self-assessment**

How well are you performing today as a strategic thinker? It's time to think about it! Give yourself an honest check to consider how much time and energy you focus on figuring out what the future holds for you and your organization.

Rate yourself using the following scale:
0: Never, 1: Occasionally, 2: Often, 3: Always

| Strategic thinking—self-assessment | | | | |
|---|---|---|---|---|
| I take the time to gather diverse information that might impact the future of my business. | 0 | 1 | 2 | 3 |
| I organize and analyze the information I collect, to identify patterns and trends. | 0 | 1 | 2 | 3 |
| I develop and explore future scenarios that might emerge for my organization. | 0 | 1 | 2 | 3 |
| I socialize my thinking to refine it and decide what we should be doing now. | 0 | 1 | 2 | 3 |
| Total score | | | | |

If you scored 9 or greater, you're doing a solid job thinking and strategizing about what the future holds for your organization. If you rated yourself 6–8, you might need to set aside time to more deliberately think about the trends that affect your organization. If you scored yourself 5 or below, you're focusing most of your time on operations and could be missing the big picture.

If strategic thinking is a gap for you, keep reading. We have a few thoughts on how to close it.

## Strategic thinking defined

Here's a definition of strategic thinking from Harvard Business Review's "HBR Guide to Thinking Strategically":[1] "Strategic thinking is about analyzing problems and opportunities from a broad perspective and understanding the impact your actions have on others. Strategic thinkers visualize what might or could be and take a holistic approach to day-to-day issues and challenges."

One way to put strategic thinking into perspective is to look around your organization and find people who are effective strategic thinkers. Observe them. Watch what they do and how they interact with others. Ideally in a forum such as a meeting or a business review, consider how they communicate their thoughts (and as important, what they are thinking). How does it differ from what other people do and say?

You will find a set of behaviors that distinguishes those people apart from their peers. They often ask probing questions, trying to understand issues and opportunities that may not be readily apparent to everyone else. They're able to think across time periods, linking information from the past and the present with foresight about the future. They are also able to think adaptively, adjusting their goals and plans to situations as they present themselves.

While you may not be the next Elon Musk or Howard Schultz, by watching others, you can improve the way you approach your work and refine your own strategic thinking skills.

## Skill builder One: GAPS strategic thinking process

Even after you've watched others doing it well, it can seem daunting to try and turn yourself into a brilliant strategic thinker. That's why we've streamlined the process of thinking about strategy into four simple steps.

Here is our four-step GAPS system for building your strategic thinking skills:

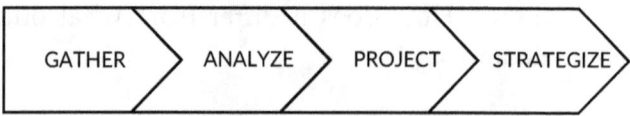

1. **Gather:** Find and assemble data from a variety of sources, not just the readily available information about your environment and your organization's strategy.

2. **Analyze:** Structure and explore data until you can spot emerging patterns and generate new insights.

3. **Project:** Imagine what the future could hold. How will various possible scenarios affect your company?

4. **Strategize:** Identify the decisions and actions that need to be made now. Consult your data, consider trends, and lean into others' wisdom in setting your strategy.

If these steps seem like a departure from your day-to-day work, that's good. Strategic thinking isn't something that takes place as part of your normal routines. It often requires the habit of setting aside time for quiet thought and independent reflection.

Now let's discuss each step of the process in detail.

## Gather

To become an insightful strategic thinker, you need to know what's happening inside your organization, within your competitive landscape, and in the wider world. You need to pull together a complete inside and outside view. One challenge to good strategic thinking is that many leaders gather limited information, usually from a handful of familiar sources, without a true understanding of what they are searching for. This is a mistake. It channels you into looking at issues in prefabricated ways, which may be different from how you would conclude on your own. By contrast, the effective strategic thinker looks more broadly for information and even seeks out conflicting data. That might seem strange, but in the words of famed US Army General George Patton: "If everyone is thinking the same thing, someone isn't thinking." Don't let that someone be you. Create a detailed picture of your landscape by regularly gathering data from a variety of sources.

Where to start? Where can you find information—general and specific—that will help you in piecing together a composite picture of your business reality? As peculiar as it might sound, gathering useful information begins with asking the right questions.

### Ask the right questions

In her article "4 Ways to Improve Your Strategic Thinking Skills," leadership development consultant Nina Bowman offers direct advice on asking the right questions.[2] "You can practice using strategic thinking by asking yourself, 'How do I broaden what I consider?'" She also notes, "Questions are the language of strategy."

As simple as this sounds, many leaders don't ask hard questions that reveal critical knowledge gaps—gaps that can be filled by collecting the right information.

Asking useful questions requires starting with some straightforward inquiries—the kind the busy, operations-focused manager can overlook. Executive coach and Harvard Business Review (HBR) author Lisa Lai lists five questions in her article "Being a Strategic Leader is About Asking the Right Questions," which provide a great baseline for getting started.

1. **What are we doing today?** This requires understanding the full scope of work you and your team are currently working on.

2. **Why are you doing the work you're doing? Why now?** The work you're doing at any point should represent your highest priorities and should reflect the best use of your time.

3. **How does what we're doing today align with the bigger picture?** It's vital that you know how your actions support the key objectives for your organization and align the broader changes happening in the external environment.

4. **What does success look like for our team?** As important the work itself is, you need to know what the outcomes are that you're trying to achieve for you and your team.

5. **What else could we do to achieve more, better, faster?** Over time, practices, processes and performance improve. It's important to identify ways in which your own work can be done more efficiently and effectively.[3]

## *Understand your organization's strategy*

If you ask only the questions we've just posed, you'll be doing a lot more strategic thinking than most people. That's a great start, but to be truly effective as a strategic thinker, you will need a little more context—the kind that your organization's strategy provides. You need to learn the strategy of your organization.

What is strategy? In short, it's an integrated set of choices that position a company, in its operating environment, to achieve competitive advantage over the long term. That's a mouthful. A shorter definition: The set of decisions and actions company leaders make and take to win in their business, however they define winning.

Sometimes, if the business is small, the strategy is in the heads of the founders. More often, it's found in the strategic plan—the document that highlights the priorities, goals, initiatives, and investments the organization is making in the short to medium term. If your company is large, and you don't have immediate access to the strategic plan, public company information such as 10-Ks, analyst reports, and earnings calls can be rich sources of information about a business's strategy. They're also a great way to gain insights into the broader operating environment. Regardless of how you access your company's strategy, understanding it is an essential part of the strategic thinking process.

## Scan the landscape

Exploring your own work and assessing how it fits into your organization's strategy builds a solid strategic thinking foundation. To be truly effective, though, you need to go beyond information that's readily available. You need to expand your field of vision and examine the environment outside of your company's four walls.

Strategic thinkers ask questions like:

- What trends are occurring in our environment, arena, or industry?

- What will be the impact of key trends in the future on our industry, our customers, our competitors, our business, our partners, *and our employees?*

- *What should we be doing now to prepare ourselves for the effects of trends?*

These questions are simple; uncovering answers to them is more challenging. Addressing the questions well requires regularly gathering data that at first blush may not seem useful or even relevant. In some cases, the information you collect may even be contradictory. Don't panic—that's OK and, in fact, you should expect it. The wider you cast your net and the more information you assemble, the more frequently you will encounter conflicting information. Your job will be to make sense of it and develop a point of view about what the future holds for your industry, your business, your team, and even yourself. That's the essence of strategic thinking—having a good understanding of what the future might hold, and how you and your organization fit within it.

---

### EXAMPLE: Peloton

Nine years before COVID-19 hit, the founders of Peloton scanned the landscape of the existing exercise industry and saw two worlds. There was home-gym equipment you could use all alone; and there were expensive memberships for gyms where you could go and take classes.

Peloton brought these two worlds together in a new way: People could exercise privately, at home, and on their own schedule, while connected online to motivating class instructors and supportive peers.

Peloton struggled to find funding for this hybrid idea. Software investors didn't like that the customer had to buy a physical bike, while hardware-focused venture capitalists didn't get the online aspect. The team persisted, selling its first handful of bikes on Black Friday 2013.

Having read the marketplace signals on how the fitness industry could better serve people's needs, Peloton was perfectly positioned to explode when the pandemic hit. Suddenly, maintaining fitness and mental health in isolation was a top priority for many. By 2021, Peloton had grown to 3.6 million subscribers.[4]

Sadly, managers didn't keep up their data gathering and trend-scanning, and by 2022, Peloton was in trouble due to equipment oversupply and slowing demand.[5] They're now regrouping.

---

One final thought on gathering information: Be sure you don't overlook information sources from within your own company. Employee surveys, management reports, and commentaries as well as informal insights from discussion groups can be a rich source of information. Seek them out and use them as part of your reviews. The information you find might be enlightening.

Once you've cast your net wide and assembled your data, you can begin the process of making sense of what it's telling you. You'll address that in the next step of the process—analyze your data to understand trends and assess their potential impact.

## Analyze

If you've done a good job gathering data, you may feel a bit overwhelmed by what you've assembled.

Articles, research papers, opinion pieces, and raw data can easily blend into an alphabet soup of information that doesn't seem like it will ever generate any insights. However, if you've looked at the raw data, you probably have a few initial thoughts about the future from your initial scanning, and now you need to turn those initial ideas into an informed point of view. That requires a little more thinking about what you're looking for, after which it becomes a lot easier to detect patterns and spot the trends that will shape your strategic viewpoints.

### Determine what you want to know

In Lewis Carroll's famed book *Alice in Wonderland*, Alice—amidst her travels—asks the Cheshire Cat a simple question: "Would you tell me please which way I ought to go from here?" "That depends a good deal on where you want to get to," replies the cat. "I don't much care," says Alice, to which the Cheshire Cat replies, "Then it doesn't much matter which way you go."

It's the same with the data and information you've collected—if you don't know what you're looking for, any analysis will suffice. You will learn something, but you won't uncover what you really want to know.

Maybe you're interested in whether the market for your product will continue to grow, or if there are new products on the horizon that will impact that. Perhaps you want to get a better understanding of how customers' needs are evolving. You may be focused on supply for a key input—some technology component such as a microprocessor. Questions like these serve as the starting point for interrogating your data.

Here are few other joggers to get you started:

- How will emerging trends affect our business?
- What's the biggest risk to our business today? Five years from today?
- What's the most damaging thing that could happen to our company?
- What are our immediate competitors doing?
- What companies could become competitors that aren't currently?
- What technology has the potential to dramatically alter how we create products or deliver services?

There may be other specific questions you'd like to add, based on what you see in your data, but these will get you started. Create different questions as your situation dictates, and be sure to change or alter them as needed.

### Zooming in and out

Many leaders worry they'll overlook some issue in their analysis, which will ultimately lead to a wrong conclusion or a bad decision. This fear can lead to analysis paralysis and ultimately impact the usefulness of the analysis effort. One way to prevent this from happening is to explore your data from different perspectives. Think of it as looking at the data through different camera lenses. Some shots are up close, while others are far away. Harvard Business School professor Rosabeth Moss Kanter describes this as zooming out and zooming in. Start with as wide-angle a lens as possible. Try to grasp the big picture. From there, gradually move closer from the external environment to your industry, to competitors, ending with the view inside your company.[6]

Many leaders get stuck in a viewpoint that's only zoomed out or zoomed in, Kanter notes. It's the rare leader who excels at analyzing information across the spectrum. Strive to continually increase the range of your zoom lens, and you will gain greater insights into the information you're examining.

### Identify relationships and patterns

As you look at trends, you'll probably see patterns emerge. This is the heart of analysis: Seeing the relationships between your data points. Let's say your information gathering has yielded the fact that three of your competitors have withdrawn from a similar product line in favor of new, higher-ticket items. Or perhaps they're preparing to exit a market. At the same time, you've spotted a new technology all of them have adopted—in fact, one of your competitors has announced an acquisition of a small company that is a pioneer in the technology you've identified. This might lead you to believe you're onto something important.

One company's move might well be an anomaly, but three make a trend. Your first thought might be that your company needs to rapidly follow the lead of the organization making the acquisition. Your new insight might also point to opportunities for you to serve customers they've left behind. With a little more research and a few more targeted questions, you can establish an informed point of view on what's happening in your industry.

As you look at trends, be aware that everyone examines information through the filter of their own biases. It's human nature. You need to actively counter your preconceptions so you can objectively analyze your findings. Once you've gathered data and analyzed it for trends, the important task is to realize what those trends will mean to your business. History is rife with examples of companies that paid the price after failing to fully consider the impact of changes they identified to their business.

## *Mistakes to avoid during analysis*

The purpose of analysis is to bring together everything you've learned, to create a complete, coherent picture. It sounds simple, but this is where leaders struggle the most—we estimate only 20% of leaders really excel at synthesis. It's challenging, messy work that doesn't always lead to a tidy conclusion. Leaders make a few common mistakes, which—if avoided—will improve your outcomes:

- **Not enough questioning.** Look for fresh ways to analyze research that might reveal other trends. Hint: Don't rely on the executive summary of a study—there are often further trends hidden in the raw data.

- **Discarding the unexpected.** Effective synthesis involves looking for the unusual. Don't overlook what seems anomalous—that's often where the richest information lies.

- **Ignoring adjacent industries and arenas.** Most executives look only at their own industry, when related industries may have useful strategic ideas. Sometimes these are where the most dangerous threats and promising opportunities lie.

Now that you've synthesized what you've learned, let's discover how to project future scenarios to guide your strategic thinking.

## Project

Armed with insights from your analysis, and aware of trends emerging in your environment, now you can start assembling a picture of how the future might look. Worried that peering into the future is like trying to make out shapes in the passing clouds (and about as solid)? Don't be. No one expects you to be clairvoyant. The point of this part of strategic thinking is not to be perfect—it's to be directionally correct about where the world is going and how you might successfully make it there.

### Think into the future

At first glance, the future seems to be a wide-open playing field. Can anyone make sense of it? Fortunately, there are organizations that do. For example, energy companies are masters at future projection, and for good reason—it can take decades to develop oil and gas fields or construct wind farms. Other alternate energy sources take even longer. One company that goes to great lengths to consider the future is Shell Oil. While it might seem "far out," Shell has plan for net-zero emissions by 2050.[7] You can bet they consider future scenarios in which fossil fuels are banned or exhausted, and their company's fortunes rest on alternate fuels. Panasonic is still consulting a 250-year plan created by their founder, Matsushita, between the two world wars.[8] Your industry may not need to envision such a far-off future (though it can inspire some creative thinking), but you might still not be sure where to begin.

## Use the time cone

Futurist Amy Webb, founder of the Future Today Institute, says she doesn't use a traditional timeline. Instead, she uses a time cone, as shown here.

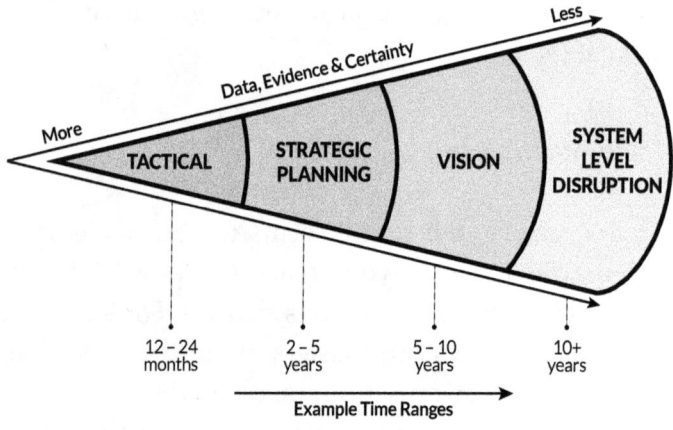

*Time cone[9]*

A common mistake when projecting time into the future comes from looking at only one point in time—say, five years from now. This boxes in thinking to just one increment. Another mistake is considering events or trends in binary terms, meaning something either will happen or it won't. However, evolution unfolds over time, and there's no guarantee a trend will play out as forecasted.

To remedy these challenges, Webb adds to the time frame several horizons that become less certain over time. Clear data and near-term, easily gathered evidence drives tactical decisions over the next twelve to twenty-four months. Longer-term, weaker signals are more strategic and potentially disruptive, but their full impact may not emerge for many years. If they come to pass, some of these trends may erase entire industries and create new ones.

Recall how an oil company might think about the future of electric vehicles. Projecting events into the future within the time cone helps you toggle between multiple time periods and gives you a more representative picture of what the future might hold. Given the speed at which the world is evolving, it's more important than ever to project *multiple* possible future scenarios. For example, under some conditions, the switch to electric vehicles might accelerate rapidly, and under other conditions, it might slow down or even stop. The time cone can be used for that as well. The goal is to create a composite that gives you and your team the best chance of creating a flexible strategy that could work well across multiple likely future scenarios. You might even avoid waking up a year or three from now to find your company is obsolete.

## TWELVE SKILLS

### *The answers to your questions*

At this point, you should begin to see answers to those fundamental questions you asked at the start of your GAPS process. Projecting into the future helps narrow down and focus the ideas you developed in the analysis phase. Your future forecasts help you see that some decisions you'd like to make might not work in fast-changing times, while others will hold great promise. Eventually, you have to decide which future seems most likely and move forward to the final step in your GAPS journey. It's time to strategize.

## Strategize

With all the information, insights, and forecasting assembled, you're ready to select the optimal strategy that will bring you success both in your current situation and in the future. Unfortunately, this is the point where many leaders head in the wrong direction. It should be an activity that charts a future direction, with key actions to get there, but strategizing is often little more than a financial spreadsheet exercise paired with a laundry list of to-dos. This approach rarely yields a coherent strategy. Remember that devising a strategy is never a step to rush through; nor is it a one and done process. This final step will determine where the organization is going, how it will win in its chosen markets, and the key initiatives that will get it there.

## *Understanding what a strategy is*

One of the longstanding problems in strategizing is that—strange but true—many leaders don't really know what a strategy is. As pointed out by Freek Vermeulen in his HBR article "Many Strategies Fail Because They're Not Actually Strategies":[10]

> "Many so-called strategies are in fact goals. 'We want to be the number one or number two in all the markets in which we operate' is one of those. It does not tell you what you are going to do; all it does is tell you what you hope the outcome will be. But you'll still need a strategy to achieve it."

To achieve whatever goals you set out to achieve, you need to determine a clear set of choices to get there, but what are those choices?

## *Components of a strategy statement*

Dave Collis from Harvard Business School notes in his HBR article, "Why Do So Many Strategies Fail?"[11] on the components of a good strategy:

> "It requires making carefully coordinated choices about the opportunities to pursue; the business model with the highest potential to create value; how to capture as much of that value as possible; and the implementation

processes that help a firm adapt activities and build capabilities that allow it to realize long-term value."

Let's look at each element in turn.

Ask a strategy professional what strategy really is, and they'll likely tell you it all boils down to one word: Choices. Which choices constitute a strategy, though?

According to researchers Collis and Rukstad, there are three primary decisions that comprise what they dub a strategy statement:

- **Objective:** A single, precise objective that will drive the firm over the coming few years (such as reach a certain revenue level or achieve a prescribed market share).

- **Scope:** Scope comprises three elements: customer and/or product/service offering, geographic area and level of vertical integration. A good scope should help define what a firm should do or not do.

- **Advantage:** Consists of two parts: The firm's value proposition (how it creates value for customers) and the unique activities that help the firm delivery on the value proposition.[12]

Another important point: The authors note that the statement should be no longer than thirty-five words.

Sound simple? It's not. As an illustration, here's the one we use for our company, CLIR Coaching:

"To grow to 25 client programs in 2025 by offering Twelve Skills capability building programs to results-focused, high-growth clients who want to develop a robust pipeline of promotion ready leaders."

Whether you work for a small or large organization; in an internal function or an external, customer-facing unit, the strategy statement is an effective tool to focus your efforts and motivate your team.

It's tempting to stop thinking about strategy once the strategy statement is complete. That said, you might be wondering, *Well, if that's not enough, what else is there?* The strategy statement is great at specifying where you're going, with whom and where you'll compete, and how you'll win, but only at a high level. You need more detail to build a strategy you can execute. That's where the business model comes in, which is covered in detail in Chapter 11.

### *Implementation process*

The final piece of strategizing comes from identifying which major projects the company will undertake (and complete) to drive the business forward. These are called *strategic initiatives* because they are aligned specifically with key elements of the business model. For example, if a piece of your strategy depends on developing and rolling out new products, you may need a strategic initiative to revamp the new-product development process. Because projects consume so many resources, be careful how you create and manage them.

Barrows and Neely list seven essential factors for success:

1. Focus on business value, not technical detail.
2. Establish clear accountability for results.
3. Have a consistent process for managing unambiguous checkpoints.
4. Have a clear methodology for planning and executing projects.
5. Include customers at the beginning of the project and involve them as things change.
6. Manage and motivate people so that project efforts will experience a zone of optimal performance.
7. Provide the project team members the tools and techniques they need to produce consistently successful projects.[13]

Before you engage in a laundry list of projects, be sure to prioritize them to your most important objectives. Derek Lidow suggests putting each of your projects into one of these categories:

- Critical—if this doesn't happen now, it's over
- Important—really should happen, but you could survive a while without
- Desirable—your "wanna haves"[14]

This process should help winnow your list and reveal the top priorities.

## Getting started with strategic thinking

In this chapter you learned our four-step GAPS method for becoming a great strategic thinker: Gather, Analyze, Project, and Strategize. You also learned the elements of a strategy and discovered the barriers that prevent many leaders from becoming good strategists, and how to overcome those barriers.

Are you ready to make strategic thinking part of your regular routine? Here are a few tips to make it happen:

- **Make the time.** Create a sacrosanct, regular appointment on your calendar for strategic planning.
- **Create a place.** Whether it's from a little-used, small conference room at the office; in the shower; or on your morning walk, find a location where you can regularly work on your GAPS steps.

- **Keep it separate.** Strategic thinking happens in a different part of the brain from operational thinking. Don't try to do both types at the same time.

- **Delegate data gathering.** Recruit help in gathering information—it's the one part of this process you don't have to do yourself.

- **Make it a routine.** Trend spotting requires reviewing data over time. Consider setting regular strategy meetings, where team members convene to review data and brainstorm ideas.

The most important step of all: Begin. Don't let day-to-day operational challenges crowd out strategic thinking time. Without robust strategic plans, those operational challenges will only grow over time. With your GAPS method for strategic thinking and your resources in hand, you're ready to move on to the next step: Using your strategy skills to solve business problems that arise in your organization. That's what we'll cover in the next chapter.

# 2
# Unlocking Problem Solving

Operating a business is never a smooth ride. Problems crop up from the moment the doors open. Worse, the sources of problems can seem endless: New competitors, changes in economic conditions, technology shifts, hiring and firing of employees, lawsuits, cash crunches, new regulations, etc. You can see from our short and incomplete list that businesses have plenty of problems. That means leaders do too. That's why they need to know how to effectively think about and solve problems. In this chapter we shift from understanding strategy to a skill closely related to it: Problem solving.

## Why problem solving?

You might be wondering, *Don't most leaders learn how to solve problems early in their careers? Why would this be one of the Twelve Skills when it seems so basic?* Good questions, but let's think them through.

First, there is a difference between solving a problem and solving a problem well. Remember when you took a multiple choice test? Hopefully, you recall the common test-taking strategy of eliminating obvious wrong answer choices and selecting from the set of remaining alternatives. This approach increases scores, but students don't use it. Even the simplest process, consistently used, will improve outcomes. More importantly, as you progress through roles of increasing responsibility, the problems you face become more challenging. Easy problems get fixed long before they reach your desk; you're stuck with the ones other people can't solve. You need much stronger skills now. Finally, top managers seek out people who can fix problems. Leaders who calmly analyze situations and guide their team to solutions attract attention and put themselves on the fast track to advancement.

With that in mind, this chapter will show you how to figure out what your problems are and how to craft good solutions. That may sound funny—figuring out what your problems are—but as one of our consulting colleagues used to say, "Whenever we talked to executives and they told us what was causing their problems, we always assumed they were wrong."

That may sound arrogant, but if the leaders describing their problems knew how to fix them, they wouldn't be hiring consultants in the first place.

---

**EXAMPLE: Beverage company**

One of us consulted with a global beverage company that strived for 99.9% quality. They had a quality problem with the little "neck" labels that go around the skinny tops of their glass bottles. The labels faded, they got wet and peeled, and little bits of neck label stuck to customers' fingers. Gross.

Hours were spent in team meetings, discussing the best way to fix what they called the "neck label quality problem." Should the label be a different shape that would be less prone to peeling? Could they use a different adhesive? Many ways were offered to solve the problem.

Meanwhile, customer surveys showed that drinkers flat out disliked the neck labels. They didn't want the labels improved—they wanted them *gone*. The company's biggest problem wasn't really that customers found their neck label annoying—it was that they were putting the label on the bottle in the first place.

Ironically, this was a problem that could be solved easily in a way that saved manufacturing time and costs. However, since the problem was originally formulated to improve the neck label, the team working on the issue missed that solution entirely. As the decades-old quality management rule states: There's no point improving something that shouldn't be done at all.

---

Is this beverage company's flub a fluke? No. In fact, most companies misidentify their problem, says Dwayne Spradlin, founder of the problem-solving marketplace InnoCentive.[15] We all tend to see problems from our own narrow viewpoint. The bottle-factory managers could only envision tweaking their process, not eliminating an entire manufacturing step.

## Chapter goals

In this chapter we're going to help you not only define but also solve your business problem, with a simple, step-by-step process that you can apply anytime, anywhere. It will help you think about your challenges in a structured way and work toward solutions in a systematic manner. Using this process will keep you from wasting resources on actions and initiatives that don't solve your real problem.

By the end of this chapter, you will be able to:

- Examine in new and novel ways the problems you and your team face
- Apply critical thinking to poorly defined issues
- Use a structured process to increase the odds you'll reach a favorable solution
- Strengthen your ability to help colleagues solve their challenges

**EXERCISE: Problem solving—self-assessment**

Maybe you're already an ace problem solver; maybe not. To get started, let's take a look at how you solve problems currently.

Rate yourself using the following scale:
0: Never, 1: Occasionally, 2: Often, 3: Always

| Problem solving—self-assessment | | | | |
|---|---|---|---|---|
| I take the time to clearly define problems. | 0 | 1 | 2 | 3 |
| I break problems down into all possible component causes. | 0 | 1 | 2 | 3 |
| I analyze the potential component causes of problems. | 0 | 1 | 2 | 3 |
| I choose the best action to address the problem's cause and follow through. | 0 | 1 | 2 | 3 |
| Total score | | | | |

If you scored 9 or greater, you have a solid grasp of problem solving. If you found yourself in the 6 to 8 range, there's room to make some improvements. If you rated yourself 5 or below, this chapter is definitely for you. The good news is, that's why you're here.

Now let's introduce a simple process that you can follow to improve your problem-solving skills in any situation.

## Problem solving defined

Before we delve into our problem-solving model, let's be sure we understand what a problem is. A problem is the difference between the existing state and the desired state. Dissatisfaction comes from the gap between where you are and where you want to be. For example, if your project is running late—bonus points if you have a project plan that tells you how late you are—the problem is the difference between where you are now (the current state) and being on schedule (the desired state). Problem solving is the process of figuring out how to close the gap to get back on track.

## Skill builder Two: D2A2 problem-solving process

Many problems aren't as simple to describe as a project running late. To think through more complex challenges, your task will be a whole lot easier when you use a process. Our approach to problem solving boils the process down to four simple, well-defined steps.

The problem-solving steps are:

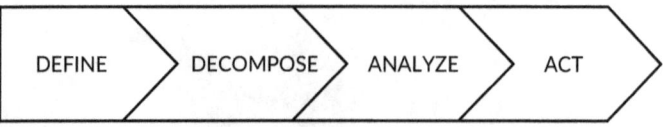

1. **Define:** Define the problem as clearly as possible.

2. **Decompose:** Break the problem down into a set of potential causes.

3. **Analyze:** As carefully as possible, analyze the different potential causes.

4. **Act:** Choose the best action to address the main challenge.

Don't let the simplicity of these steps fool you. Poor problem solvers skip over them if they even consider them at all. Let's work through each step in some detail.

## Define

To solve a problem, you first need to know what that problem is. As simple as this sounds, few managers do. In surveys of more than 100 C-Suite executives worldwide, 85% said their companies were bad at problem diagnosis, says Thomas Wedell-Wedellsborg, author of "What's Your Problem?"[16] Think about that for a minute. If more than three out of four organizations are poor at figuring out what the problem is, imagine how many teams are working on the wrong problems. This is why it's so critical to take the time—either individually or on your team—to determine as accurately as possible what problem you are trying to solve.

**TWELVE SKILLS**

*Frame and reframe the problem*

To zero in on your most urgent problem, you need to look at your challenge from several different angles. Think of yourself as a photographer, trying many different camera lenses to get different viewpoints. The photographer might start with a closeup of a small detail—say, an apple on a picnic blanket. Then they might slowly reframe until they're seeing that picnic blanket from space, with the dark void all around and the curve of the Earth visible.

Different framing often recasts the problem and points leaders and teams toward different solutions. Wedell-Wedellsborg uses the example of an aging apartment building, where the tenants complain that the ancient elevator is too slow, so some residents are threatening to move out. The quick problem that many people rush to solve is the elevator needing to be faster. From this formulation, ideas such as *replace the elevator with a new one* or *install a more powerful motor* pop out almost instantly, but taking the time to reframe the problem suggests other solutions. Changing the problem to needing to make waiting for the elevator less annoying yields a different solution, focused on making the wait less tedious. Now this problem can be solved by playing music over a sound system, putting up a television screen that plays music videos, moving mailboxes nearer the elevator, or installing mirrors so people can check their appearance while they wait. These options are far cheaper than a new elevator and might end the tenant complaints.

To reframe your problems, Wedell-Wedellsborg suggests a seven-step process:

1. **Get buy-in:** All parties have to agree to reframe the problem, or the reframing exercise is pointless.

2. **Bring outsiders:** Find fresh voices, either inside the company or from other stakeholders. Include those with contrarian or outlying viewpoints—it can be useful to find people who outright disagree.

3. **Get definitions in writing:** Create a written statement that defines the problem. This ensures group agreement.

4. **Ask what's left out:** Think about what's encompassed in your definition—and what may be missing.

5. **Find your type:** Can you categorize your problem as one of operations, PR, transportation, or human resources? Each category would suggest different solutions.

6. **Consider positive exceptions:** Look for times when the stated problem didn't occur. What was different?

7. **Find out if there are different objectives:** Various stakeholders may have different goals that each suggest new solutions.[17]

Step 3, writing a problem statement, is a critical activity to master for effective problem solving. Let's look at this task in depth.

## *Inside the problem statement*

Good problem statements are simple, yet most managers struggle to create them. Creating a well-defined problem statement is critical; as a spin on the old saying: A problem well stated is a problem half solved. To begin with, defining a problem in writing starts your mind turning on possible solutions. It also involves people—ideally your team—in the problem-solving process. It helps inculcate the discipline of thinking in a structured way about the problem too.

What makes a good problem statement? To start, it's succinct—nothing too wordy or elaborate. It should define a clear goal or outcome for resolving the problem. Most importantly, it doesn't talk about solutions—we're not there yet.

You might be wondering, *If it doesn't have solutions, what does the problem statement say?* In short, it should:

- Describe what's important about the issue
- Depict what a successful outcome would look like and identify the gap between the current state and the desired one

- Be measurable
- Avoid getting into solutions

Conversely, poor problem statements fail to formulate the problem clearly. They don't add context that helps improve the tangibility of the problem. In some cases, the problem statement's author sneaks their preferred solution into the statement itself. Often, initial review defines the problem as too big to readily solve.

A good problem statement helps frame the issue at a level that can be worked on. Writing a good problem statement can help you scope down to a more easily resolvable initial challenge.

Let's contrast the good and the poor with a few examples. Poor problem statements are too general and don't speak to the importance of the issue; there isn't enough substance to get your arms around the problem.

Going back to our elevator problem, here are a couple of ways the issue could be framed:

1. **Poor example:** The elevator is too slow.
2. **Poor example:** The sensor isn't working.

What's the difficulty with these examples? If you're thinking there's not much to them, you're right. They don't provide any background information to guide those working on the problem. Further, they're crafted in a way that points at a single, specific solution such as *speed up the elevator* or *replace the sensor*. There may be more to the problem, though. Let's look at the poor examples, reframed:

1. **Good example:** Tenants in the building are concerned that the elevator, given its age, is too slow. They are spending excessive time waiting for the elevator, especially during peak times of day.

2. **Good example:** The elevator is not stopping on the first floor that calls for the elevator. Residents note the elevator makes one to two stops before reaching the floor it is first called to.

These examples spotlight where many statements go wrong and how to craft a strong, useful problem statement. In both illustrations of good examples, not only is context provided, but they are written in such a way that doesn't immediately suggest a solution. This is the essence of effective problem design—teeing up the problem in a way that provides the freedom to explore solutions from different avenues. As Peter Bregman, of Bregman Partners, puts it, "If you are caught in a problem that seems unsolvable, ask this simple question: If the problem you're trying to solve weren't the problem, what else might be?"[18]

Once you've written your problem statement, it's time to test it out. Show it to people who weren't involved in creating it, to solicit their input. Find out what they think and see if they have questions. Does it seem clear? Are there bits of information missing that would be useful to include? Now is the time to encourage diverse thinkers to weigh in. Challenge them to find smaller problems within your stated one that might need to be addressed first.

Once you've tested your problem statement, it's time to start working on a solution.

## Decompose

As you draft problem statements, solutions are likely to bubble up in your mind. You'll find that the more people you share the statement with, the more ideas will be generated to address the challenge. The good news at this point is that you will have a list of potential causes and corresponding solutions to choose from; but how do you pick?

Not so fast. It's tempting to look over the set you have, pick the one that seems the most likely cause, and start executing. Don't do that yet. Despite having a list of causes, you may not have the most likely cause on your hands—more digging might be required to find it. Even if you have identified the most likely *driver* of the problem, that doesn't mean you can solve it—some additional work might be required to ensure it's a solvable challenge.

Decomposing and sorting the problem into parts helps you track your problem down to its root cause. It also gives you confidence that your chosen solution is the right one. The way to approach the most likely cause and its related solution is using a logic tree.

*Using logic trees*

Logic trees are the most effective way to help you diagram all possible causes of a problem (more on how you get to all possible solutions a bit later). When you depict a problem's causes visually, it helps you see what's behind the problem you're working on. If you're not familiar with a logic tree, it looks like the playoff brackets for March Madness, only in reverse. The start of the tree is a single point—your problem—and from there, the branches of the tree depict the various potential causes to your challenge.

Here's a simple logic tree, using our elevator challenge again and our reframed problem statement to start the build. Here's how we might look at the problem:

**UNLOCKING PROBLEM SOLVING**

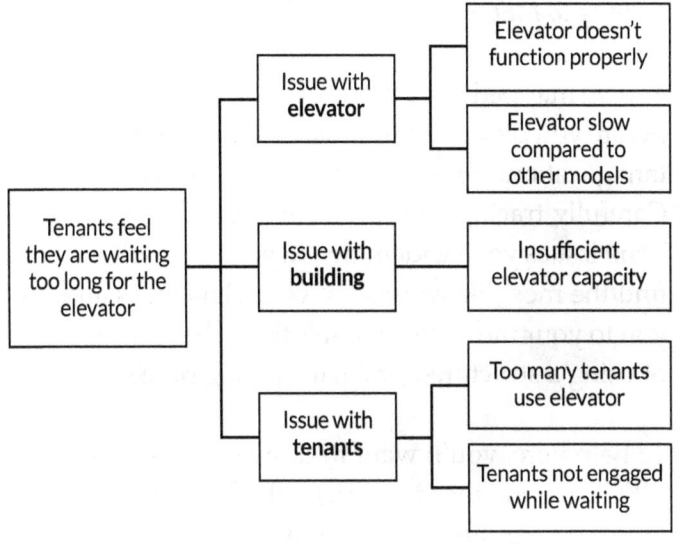

*Logic tree*

The tree begins on the left and grows to the right step by step, breaking the problem down into branches that show potential causes. You need to think like a detective as you build your tree, uncovering each potential cause like a piece of a puzzle. Keep in mind, there is no one *right* way to build a logic tree—try different approaches and test different ideas. Part of the fun comes from building logic trees with teams. It's a great way to get everyone's analytical juices flowing.

Thinking carefully through the causes will point you in the right direction of solutions, but before you do that, you need to be sure your tree contains the all the branches it needs to bear fruit.

## Getting to MECE

You've mapped out a range of causes to your problem. Before you pick one, take a step back and ask an important question: *Have we identified all the important causes?* Carefully tracing your problem through *all* the underlying issues you've identified in your tree will help you find the most likely cause of your challenges and lead you to your most effective solution. That's the purpose of using a structured problem-solving process.

To help here, you'll want to draw on a concept called MECE (pronounced *me-see*), which is shorthand for mutually exclusive, collectively exhaustive. You want to keep working on your tree until you have a tree that is both mutually exclusive and collectively exhaustive. Let's explain what that means. First, the causes you put into your tree are all different from one another (mutually exclusive). Second, taken together, they reflect every possible cause (collectively exhaustive). One of the first female Harvard MBAs, Barbara Minto, developed this groundbreaking way of thinking several decades ago.

To understand how MECE works, let's consider a simple example. You go to the doctor, complaining of pain in your chest and worried you might be having a heart attack. The doctor takes your temperature, looks in your ear, and says, "I've seen this before and I know exactly what your problem is. You need a triple bypass—stat!" After you recover from the initial shock, two things cross your mind. First, you need a second opinion (as well as a new doctor). Second, you'd really like your next doctor to conduct a more thorough exam. While you may not have taken the Hippocratic oath, even you know giving a diagnosis without a full examination is medical malpractice. Remember, it's malpractice in management too.

This diagnosis is *not* MECE. Your symptom is chest pain. Dozens of conditions can cause that: Panic attack, pancreatitis, indigestion, and so on. A MECE diagnosis would lay out a set of possible causes and then eliminate some or most of them by taking a detailed medical history and running tests. Your doctor should think about mutually exclusive causes—that is, separate from each other and not connected by some common factor. The list also needs to be collectively exhaustive—that is, you need to consider all the reasonable alternatives to a heart attack. Your doctor's diagnosis doesn't pass either of those tests, so it's not MECE at all.

## Analyze

Let's fast-forward to when you have a clearly defined problem, along with set of distinctly different but comprehensive (MECE) potential causes of the problem. The key point to remember here is they are *potential* causes. To figure out the actual cause, you will need to perform some type of analysis. In the example of chest pain, this is where the doctor runs tests on all the potential causes of the pain to rule out those things that are not problems, leaving the single one that is most likely the source.

## *Root cause analysis*

Root cause methods rely on a basic assumption: The first problem we see is often not the one we should (or can) solve. Real-world problems often have underlying causes that we need to discover, similar to how a plant is connected to a root beneath the soil.

One well-known technique for finding the root cause of a problem began at Toyota. Taiichi Ohno, former architect of the Toyota Production System, recognized that to track a problem back to its root cause, you need to ask *Why?* five successive times. By the fifth time, you move beyond symptoms and find the root cause.[19] To use the five whys method,[20] stick to the simple facts of the problem you're working on.

For instance, let's say your company has a shortage of frontline employees. Using the five whys might look like this:

1. **Why do we lack sufficient frontline workers?** Our staff turnover is high.

2. **Why?** This is not a great place to work.

3. **Why?** Our compensation packages are inferior.

4. **Why?** Our pay is on par with competitors, but our benefits are worse.

5. **Why?** We don't offer tuition reimbursement, flexible holidays, or comprehensive company-paid healthcare plans.

When you've reached the fifth why, you've hit the root cause. Now you can take action: Benchmarking and beefing up your benefits package. This should go a long way toward fixing your initial problem. Asking *Why?* enough times to arrive at your root cause guided you to the right course of action.

Remember: Don't confuse causes with symptoms. A symptom of the problem is not the problem itself. We're looking to uncover systemic issues that are causing business problems, which is going to need us to dig past what's right on the surface. You know you've asked enough whys when taking action on your answer would resolve the problem.

## Act

At this point, you need to take action and solve your problem. You have a working theory about the most viable cause and what a potential solution might be, but you need to keep a few things in mind as you do.

### *Picking the best solution*

Have you ever heard the phrase *There's more than one way to skin a cat*? There may be a few different ways to solve your problem, and you need to consider your constraints and available resources. Maybe you need a solution quickly. Perhaps you have a limited budget and need a DIY (versus outsourced) solution. Sometimes the ideal solution isn't feasible; you need to be thoughtful and creative in your approach.

In our heart example, perhaps the doctor pinpoints the source of your chest pain (based on extensive testing) as anxiety, stemming from your difficulties solving problems at work. You could quit your job immediately, but that might be a bit drastic. Perhaps adding exercise or meditation to your daily routine would be more sensible? Thinking about and even trying different approaches that fit your budget and lifestyle would probably be a good place to start.

### Check your biases

Let's face it: We all have biases in how we approach problem solving. Some people overly rely on intuition, while others rely too much on data. In either case, you should avoid relying on your usual thinking patterns. This is why you want to use a process and involve multiple people with different points of view in your problem solving. Force yourself to think differently. Look at your proposed solution from a different perspective and consider alternatives. If you keep challenging yourself to look at your solution in novel ways, you'll be amazed at what you might uncover.

*Test and learn*

It's tempting to think that by implementing your solution, you'll have a solved problem on your hands. In an ideal world, that would be the case, but we unfortunately don't live in that world. Using a process increases the likelihood you can fix your issue, but it's not a guarantee. Be prepared to cycle back through your problem-solving steps if needed.

*Communicate your change*

Once you choose a solution and the action you need to take resolve your problem, one final task remains: It's time to communicate your action plan to your team. You want to get your staff enthusiastic and motivated to work on resolving the problem together.

That's not always easy, because people hate change, and here you are likely introducing a new way of doing things. No doubt there'll be at least some resistance. For more on skillful communication in tough situations, see Chapter 4 on how to communicate clearly.

# Getting started with problem solving

In this chapter you learned our four-step D2A2 process for problem solving: Define, Decompose, Analyze, and Act. You also learned techniques that will strengthen your knowledge and approach to challenges you face.

If you want to boost your problem-solving skills, here are some things to keep in mind:

- **Think before you solve.** Many leaders advance and think they have all the experience they need to solve problems. The best leaders know they can be led astray by their intuition, so they slow down and think before they solve and act.

- **Use a process.** The best way to enhance your problem solving is to follow a process and resist the temptation to "shoot from the hip."

- **Explore different viewpoints.** Most organizations are filled with people who think differently. Be sure your process takes advantage of different perspectives and challenges traditional ways of solution thinking.

The D2A2 problem-solving process will be useless if you don't build the habit of identifying problems and finding solutions, both individually and across your organization. Find regular time in your schedule to discuss emerging issues with your team, inviting them to bring challenges forward for discussion. If your company culture is to ignore problems, employees will hesitate to bring up issues they see.

Now you've learned how to find brilliant solutions to business problems, read on for another essential skill that will make it easier to solve business problems. When you develop your executive presence, your team members will look up to you as a leader they trust and want to follow, which will make it much easier to implement your solutions.

# 3
# Enhancing Executive Presence

It used to be simple for rising executives to master the art of executive presence—all you had to do was imitate your boss. Walk like him, dress like him, talk like him, and—if you can master them—engage in the same hobbies he did (usually including golf). If you spoke, dressed, or behaved differently from your boss, you probably weren't on the fast track to promotion.

Things have evolved. Executive presence is a skill that's changed more than most over time. Where executive leaders once all seemed to fit one cookie-cutter mold—a tall Caucasian male who is good-looking, confident, and has a commanding voice—today's leaders come in all genders, ethnicities, backgrounds, beliefs, appearances; you name it. Leaders create a strong presence in a variety of ways, but most importantly by emphasizing their unique strengths and personality. Where once evolving into an organization man[21] was the goal, now tapping your authentic self[22] is the most important part of developing your own leadership brand.

As you move up, you need to decide what sort of leader you are, based on your core values and convictions. Then you need to find a way to express those beliefs and your personality in an authentic way. In other words, it's time to build your personal brand.

## Why executive presence?

When you transition from individual contributor to rising manager or leader, it's important to build your presence. The way you presented yourself as an individual contributor on a team likely won't help you advance or succeed in your first management role. Keeping your head down and your mouth closed, and doing great work aren't the hallmarks of those perceived to be effective leaders. To be effective in more senior roles, you first need those around you to begin seeing you as a leader—as someone who can motivate others, solve challenging problems, and deliver results. This is your ticket to advancement.

### EXAMPLE: Orit Gadeish

When we think of someone with great executive presence who has succeeded by building a unique personal brand, Orit Gadeish leaps to mind. She's been the chair of top consulting firm Bain & Company for years.

As if it weren't different enough to be a six-foot-tall Israeli woman who wears short skirts and chunky jewelry, as she rose to the top spot in the 1990s, Orit dyed her hair purple.[23] At a time when sporting unnatural hair color could get you dismissed from a job, Gadeish made it part of her signature look.

This wouldn't have worked for most rising executives, but it became an iconic part of her brand as a cutting-edge business thinker.

---

Gadeish's unique appearance helped communicate that she wasn't afraid to stand out. Similarly, Steve Jobs stood out with his hallmark black turtleneck. Job's personal take on dress-casual wear for one of the world's leading tech companies shows that executive presence is about being yourself, not following the herd.[24]

Business leaders need more than sheer competency to advance. If you're hoping that your hard work will eventually be rewarded with a promotion, we've got some bad news. As the research by Duke University professor and personal-branding expert Dorie Clark

**TWELVE SKILLS**

shows, highly competent executives are routinely passed over for promotion if they lack presence.[25] It's not a nice-to-have—it's a *must*-have. As a leader, you need to be more than capable—you need to inspire those around you and build trust in your decisions. Presence gives you the ability to foster that trust.

Strong executive presence is the magic ingredient that helps top managers recognize you as someone who could take on more responsibility. Think of leadership presence as you telling your team, your peers, your senior leaders—even your customers—that you are, in fact, leadership material. It's a signaling mechanism. Does this sound like acting a part? It is. The best leaders are partly actors, and you need to look and act the part in your own individual way. This helps convince others that you *are* a leader.

You need to raise your profile to be viewed as a candidate for promotion. For managers who are naturally introverted or just dislike promoting themselves, this can be a major challenge. It can feel disingenuous, and you may need some convincing. Ask yourself, *If I'm not willing or able to promote myself, who else will?* Ultimately, you need to change both your thinking and your behavior, but we know it can be done without appearing phony.

The golden rule for presence: Don't be somebody you're not. Figure out who you are, embrace it, and project that to the world. Research shows that leaders who master even just two skills (and you have twelve in this book) are seen as considerably more effective leaders that those who only focus on one.[26]

# Chapter goals

As the typical executive leader has evolved and diversified, executive presence has also been transformed. It's time to create your own powerful leadership brand.

This chapter will show you how to:

- Shape your personal style and appearance to both fit in and stand out at work

- Gain awareness of the behaviors that diminish your personal image

- Start projecting greater confidence when interacting with your colleagues

- Make a plan that continues to enhance your personal brand

---

**EXERCISE: Executive presence—self-assessment**

Before we begin, give yourself a quick test to consider how you show up today.

Rate yourself using the following scale:
0: Never, 1: Occasionally, 2: Often, 3: Always

**TWELVE SKILLS**

| Executive presence—self-assessment | | | | |
|---|---|---|---|---|
| I'm thoughtful about my appearance at work. | 0 | 1 | 2 | 3 |
| I project self-assuredness and a sense of confidence to my colleagues. | 0 | 1 | 2 | 3 |
| I communicate clearly and confidently when speaking and presenting. | 0 | 1 | 2 | 3 |
| **Total score** | | | | |

If you 7 or greater, you've got gravitas—well done. If you found yourself in the 5 or 6 category, you can make changes to show up more effectively. If you scored yourself 4 or below, you may need to pay more attention here.

Your honesty with yourself will pay off as you start investing in your presence. Realize most executives fall short in some area of presence, so if you identified a weakness, don't worry. We'll now give you insights and techniques to help you grow your executive presence.

---

## Executive presence defined

Just what is this presence that's your golden ticket to the C-Suite? Here's a short definition. In "Developing Your Leadership Presence," executive coach John Baldoni defines executive presence as earned authority.[27] "You may have a title," he notes, "but you need to earn the respect and trust of your coworkers."

Often, executives asked to define presence will come up with a single Latin word, *gravitas*, which some dictionaries define as high seriousness or solemn dignity.

John Beeson gives a more detailed definition in his article "Deconstructing Executive Presence."[28] He describes presence as: "… your ability to project mature self-confidence, a sense that you can take control of difficult, unpredictable situations; make tough decisions in a timely way and hold your own with other talented and strong-willed members of the executive team."

Think of an executive you've looked up to as a good example. A beneficial exercise is to list their leadership qualities—you'll probably see they align with the definitions above. Regardless of how you define it, you may feel you lack presence. You may have received some feedback or had an experience that made you feel like you're missing it. Good news: It can be learned. The Richard Bransons and Sheryl Sandbergs of the world didn't swagger onto the stage as the iconic leaders you know today—they developed and evolved their personas over time. You can do the same, by taking a few simple steps that will help you quickly make improvements to your leadership presence.

## Skill builder Three: ABC executive presence process

Executives can build their presence through three simple steps, as follows:

**TWELVE SKILLS**

1. **Appearance:** How you present yourself in the workplace, in terms of dress, grooming, and posture.

2. **Boldness:** Show calm, courage, and confidence in the face of challenging situations, speaking honestly even if it's uncomfortable for others.

3. **Communication:** Express your ideas clearly and confidently when you're speaking or presenting.

## Appearance

One of our seasoned coaching colleagues once attended a meeting at a major manufacturer of athletic shoes. He arrived in what he thought was appropriate business-casual attire: A checked Oxford shirt, khaki pants, a blue blazer, and tidy brown loafers. When he stopped by the office of the woman organizing the meeting, she looked at him, made an unpleasant face, and remarked that no one on the management team would take him seriously dressed like that. He was stunned. She promptly marched him down to the company store, where he bought a hooded sweatshirt, thick athletic socks, and a pair of the company's timeless high-top sneakers. Thanks to her feedback and his quick makeover, the meeting was a success.

While workplace standards for appearance have changed considerably in the past few years, there are still rules to follow so that you successfully fit in from the first and then skillfully stand out later. As Gorick Ng notes in his book *The Unspoken Rules: Secrets to Starting Your Career Off Right*, "Looking professional is all about finding the intersection of what's appropriate to your workplace and what feels authentic to you."[29]

Let's see how that works.

## Fitting in

Regardless of the setting, you need to think about how you want to appear at work. More to the point, you want to show up in ways that position you for success. To do so, pay careful attention to the details of how people in your workplace look, which should quickly give a sense of what constitutes an appropriate appearance. Maybe your office has a formal environment, due to high-profile clients with highly professional expectations, where sharp suits or dresses would be the norm. You might work for a technology or startup company where a more casual, trendy, or even youthful look is standard. Look for patterns in how people show up. For clothing, look at tops, bottoms, shoes, colors, styles, and even brands. As for accessories, get a sense for the type and kind of jewelry, handbags, briefcases, backpacks, eyewear, and the like. Be mindful of grooming in terms of hairstyle, facial hair, perfumes, colognes, and even nail

**TWELVE SKILLS**

care. Finally, don't forget body art such as tattoos or gauges. Each of these aspects of appearance matters. Together, they comprise the full picture of what is appropriate in your workplace.

Like our colleague, we've worked with many leaders who were clueless that they were dressed inappropriately. Our advice in this area is simple: Don't be one of them. Take the time to learn the norms of dress and appearance. If you're not sure you've got it right, ask a colleague or two to give you some honest, constructive feedback. It might be hard to swallow at first, but it will help you quickly figure out what does and doesn't work appearance-wise for your company.

### *Standing out*

Once you've mastered how to fit in, give some thought to the best way to stand out from peers. That might seem a strange statement: Fit in, so that once you do, you can try to look different from the rest. You just need to earn the respect and even subtle agreement of your coworkers before you can dazzle them with your appearance. You can bet Orit Gadeish didn't show up on her first day at Bain with purple hair. Only when she had mastered the inner workings of the firm and earned her colleagues' and clients' credibility as a top consultant did she have "permission" to supercharge her look as she did. Similarly, one of our coworkers, two years into her tenure, started showing up on virtual calls with colored hair and matching thick-rimmed glasses. This was a departure even for this progressive organization, yet no one questioned her. In fact, many complimented her on her bold, new look. She had earned the right to look different by doing great work and always acting like a team player.

Once you've earned your place, think about how you might stand out in ways that are true to who you are as a person. This is where you'll tap into your personal values and contrast them with those workplace standards you've come to appreciate (or at least accept for the meantime). You may reject your workplace's norms in favor of what's important to you, or you may just try to bend the rules a little as a show of your individuality. Regardless of what you do and how you go about it, be mindful of the appearance you are trying to cultivate—it will be a key component of your personal brand while you're at the organization.

### *Straightening up*

While your attire is important, it's only one aspect of appearance. There's another important element that many people overlook: Posture.

How you sit, stand, and project yourself has an impact on your overall appearance. Do you slouch when you sit, slump when you stand, or skulk when you walk? You could have the most penetrating insights, but if you deliver them from a bent and shirking position, your message won't inspire confidence. The good news is there are simple things you can do to boost your bearing.

In general, you want to project an image of confident comportment at work. Looking people straight in the eye and gesturing in a self-assured manner will help instill trust in your colleagues. People make judgments based on the look on a person's face. If the person is looking away or staring downward, the takeaway is that they lack a positive self-image—not the making of leadership material.

When giving a presentation or even just talking to coworkers, square up to your audience, stand up straight, and keep your arms down in a relaxed position at your side. Avoid putting your hands in your pocket and jingling your keys, coins, or other items that can distract. Don't lean on anything or stand with crossed legs—another sign of defensiveness and submission. When sitting, be mindful of the "computer hunch." Eliminating these habits can make a big difference to how you're perceived.

Here's a tip: Come to work every day dressed as if you're interviewing for a new job or might be called into an unexpected client meeting. How thoroughly would you vet your outfit and review your grooming to project confidence and competence in those situations? Realize that if you're hoping to be promoted, you *are* in fact auditioning for a new job. The combined effect of your appearance and posture telegraph that you're ready to move up.

## Cleaning out

One other important element, which is not directly related to your personal appearance but can impact it: The state of your workspace. It used to be that your office was your only visible workspace. People generally tolerated loose files, scattered pictures, and sundry tchotchkes in your space. Now, thanks to web meetings, people are working from home and other remote locations. This provides a window for your peers to see how you live. We've all been on video calls where a person is calling from their bedroom, where their bed is unmade and clothes are draped over the furniture. It's not a pretty sight, and it can be distracting. If a virtual background is not a possibility (which it should be), make sure you work from a space that is cleaned out and tidy, so you don't give the impression you're a slob at home. If you're forced, like so many of us are, to bring your home to work, make sure it's neat and clean for everyone's benefit—especially your own.

## Recheck your rebrand

We hope this section has given you clear ideas about how you might want to level up your dress, posture, and grooming. Maybe you're also thinking about how you could add personality to your look and stand out. Don't be afraid to put what you've learned to the test.

As you change your appearance, pay attention to see if you receive a different response from others. Be sure to ask for feedback from colleagues and mentors. If you hear your appearance isn't conveying authority, try another approach. Keep making improvements until you have a presence you feel comfortable with, and until others report that you're projecting an image of confidence and authority. That's a big part of leadership.

Now you understand the role that appearance plays in executive presence, let's look at how bold action helps build your leadership quotient.

## Boldness

Think about the boldest leader you've ever known. What were they like? How did they act? What did they do to instill confidence in others? Leaders display courage—at times even daring—and demonstrate it even when their teams are quaking inside. Leaders pull people together and make decisions under pressure, regardless of what they themselves are experiencing. They are brave in the face of adversity—willing to make a tough call and live with the results. Like it or not, this is what people want in their leaders, which is why you need to prioritize developing boldness.

In truth, boldness isn't a trait we're typically born with—it's something we have to develop over time. The sections below tease out the elements of boldness and how you can cultivate it.

## *Establish your credibility*

First and foremost, you need to establish yourself as credible. According to leadership expert Jay Conger, credibility comes from two sources: Expertise and relationships. You need to establish a firm foundation in each area if you are to be successful getting people to view you as a capable leader.[30]

Regardless of your functional capability, you want to be known as an expert in your discipline. From accounting to information technology and human resources to sales, you need to know your craft and—through your great work—persuade other people that you're a master in your domain. You need to have significant technical expertise at your disposal, because before you can be bold, your contemporaries need to believe beyond a doubt that you know what you're doing. If they don't, you will have difficulty getting buy-in for your major moves.

Remember, people initially advance in organizations because of their expertise. Demonstrating your accomplishments and those of your team reminds senior leadership of your strengths. Don't hide your experience—look for opportunities to let it shine. Your leadership credibility rests in part on the foundation stone of your experience.

While necessary, expertise alone is not enough. You need strong, long-term relationships to ensure you are viewed as a capable and trustworthy partner. We have included an entire chapter in *Twelve Skills* on building relationships, but in summary: Healthy relationships come from being a person of high integrity who is trustworthy, can be counted to deliver on their promises, and has a reputation of acting in the best interests of others and the organization.

People follow leaders, yes, but only if they trust them; and trust begins with reliability. Trusted leaders are people of their word—they announce an initiative and then make it happen. They are also people who get results. If you consistently get your projects completed on time and on budget, be sure to let people know about your accomplishments. While this can be harder than it sounds, once you practice drawing attention to your achievements, it will soon become second nature.

### *Act decisively*

Have you ever played a board or card game that required you to make a quick decision that, once made, you had to live with? For example, once you decide to roll the dice for conquering Kamchatka in Risk, you may succeed or fail, but your course is set. Leadership can be just the same—assessing situations with incomplete or conflicting pieces of information and then needing to make a decision that can't be easily reversed.

Leaders show strong presence by taking decisive action. They're willing to take a stand, even if it sometimes goes against conventional wisdom. They stick to their guns, even if the execution has some bumps. At times, you have to be willing to make difficult decisions and explain, with the courage of your convictions, why it's the right choice.

Most people have had a Domino's pizza. Founded in 1960, the company grew rapidly with a focus on fast-delivery pizza and soon became a leader in the foodservice franchise business. By the early 2000s, Domino's leadership realized they had a problem on their hands—their pizza was ranked by customers as some of the worst pizza they'd ever had. The comments gathered included: *Crust tastes like cardboard*. The new CEO—Patrick Doyle, a veteran business leader—launched a bold advertising campaign in 2010 admitting that Domino's pizza was bad and committing to doing whatever it took to turn the company's food (and reputation) around. The campaign succeeded, launching Domino's on a successful growth trajectory.

This was one of the boldest business moves of all time, and it was a gamble that paid off. Certainly, Doyle's background and expertise figured into his success but, more importantly, he took a novel and risky approach to addressing the company's challenged situation.

Doyle is now admired for his leadership skills and is viewed as someone who can successfully turn around companies—all stemming from one decisive decision. His choices affected thousands of employees and countless customers around the world.

Don't be afraid, when the time is right, to make a decisive call. Work your way up to it by establishing your credibility and building relationships. Be sure to consider the people your decisions impact, both before and after your bold action. Ask your team for their input and reactions, and hear their thoughts and feelings. Learn from them, consider their input, and let them know they've been heard.

## Communication

Communicating well at work is so important that it isn't just one of the three elements of our model for building leadership presence—it takes up the entire next chapter of this book. In this chapter we're spotlighting four essential communication components that directly impact executive presence. These are especially important for new, rising managers.

### *Speak clearly*

We've not met anyone who thinks they're unclear when they speak. However, given the verbal confusion we've experienced in meetings and presentations, clearly not everyone is clear. Adapting your speaking approach for maximum impact doesn't take much work—a few basic principles will make a monumental difference when communicating verbally.

## Remove filler words

Toastmasters is an international nonprofit educational organization, which teaches public speaking. One of the first rules they teach is to eliminate the filler words that most people aren't even aware of when they speak. Words such as *um, ah, you know* and *like* are commonplace, even among seasoned leaders. They add no value at all; worse, they bother listeners. Remove them, and the quality of your discussions will immediately improve.

## From pacing to pauses

The most effective speakers know that a monotone talk, given at the same pace without any pauses, is a sure-fire way to lose your audience's attention. To engage listeners, effective spoken communication varies the speed of the delivery. To emphasize an important point, the speaker... will... slow... down. Likewise, to maintain interest during a lively story, the speaker may speed up, adding a sense of excitement to the tale. Then the speaker may offer a long silence to let the gravity of a critical point sink in. While there is not one perfect way to build credibility when speaking, leaders need to be mindful of how their speech is impacting listeners. Asking someone to listen in to a practice session, or recording yourself and playing it back, can effectively improve both your pacing and pauses. Practice this skill, like the elimination of filler words, and the quality of your communication and leadership presence will grow.

## *Display confidence*

There are few jobs in the world as high-stakes as military special forces. Their extensive and exhausting training regimens prepare their personnel to operate in some of the most stressful situations and inhospitable environments in the world. The US Navy SEALs—perhaps the most renowned of all special forces—use a saying within their teams: *Calm is contagious.*

When leaders display poise and confidence in difficult situations, it conveys a feeling that the situation is under control and things are going to work out. During the most stressful times, however impossible it may seem to others, leaders need to project gravitas—that solemn dignity that reassures others you are in control. The world may be falling apart, but you're not. Emotional outbursts of any kind, from tears to shouting, undermine your authority and can spread panic through the ranks. Remember, your team is looking to you for calm assurance that things will be fine.

People recognize and respect people who stay calm in a crisis. Even if all you can tell them is, "We're still gathering information about this, and we'll announce our plans shortly," they'll remember that you were unflappable. People who behave like this put themselves in position for greater responsibility in their organizations. In short, they've shown that, no matter how hot it gets, they'll be comfortable in the kitchen.

## Getting started with executive presence

Showing up more confidently with your colleagues will result from the three-step ABC executive presence process: Appearance, Boldness, and Communication. Regardless of how far out of your comfort zone you feel at the outset, your skills in this area are within reach.

Here are ways to jump start your development:

- **Look in the mirror.** Solicit feedback about how you look and act, and you will find a trove of tips that will get you moving in the right direction.

- **Make a presence plan.** Make a list of ideas. Prioritize changes you think could make the biggest improvements. As you work on revamping your personal brand, don't forget to continue to ask trusted colleagues for feedback, to make sure you're on the right track.

- **Cultivate presence.** Make sure your presence fits your current role and, more importantly, the roles you want in the future. Leave people with the

**TWELVE SKILLS**

impression you are every ounce the leader they need you to be.

As with all our leadership skills, developing presence takes a time commitment. You need to set aside time in your schedule to focus on presence, perhaps making an appointment with a wardrobe consultant or a speaking coach.

In this chapter you've discovered specific ideas that will help you improve how you look. In the next chapter we'll dig deeper into communication to ensure your message matches your image.

# 4
# Developing Clear Messaging

You may be the most gifted business thinker on the planet and project a powerful image at work, but if you're tongue-tied or ham-handed when it comes to communicating your ideas to others, you're going to have a hard time moving up the ranks as a leader. That's why clear communication is one of the Twelve Skills—it's the hallmark of effective leaders. Struggle with communication and you'll struggle as a leader; it's that simple.

Even though we communicate all day, every day, at work we rarely stop to think about the effect our messaging has on our teams and on our success. The challenge for many emerging leaders—especially as they progress in their careers—is that they fail to recognize communication as a core element of their overall effectiveness.

People are taught early on in their careers that the way to get ahead is to keep their heads down, work hard, and master their specific job skills. Communication falls by the wayside because it isn't a hard skill like financial acumen or technical knowledge. Consequently, they spend little time thinking about who they're communicating with and what messages they are sending. This leads to suboptimal performance as a communicator and, ultimately, as an emerging leader. Some experts therefore rank communication as the *single* most important leadership skill.

## Why clear messaging?

You may not be convinced, and you may still question the need for formality. If that is the case, consider this insight from Boris Groysberg and Michael Slind, from their Harvard Business Review article, "The Silent Killer of Big Companies": "Most leaders today recognize how dangerous it can be to take a lax approach to people management. But how many leaders appreciate the risks that come with taking a lax approach to communication management?"[31]

Perhaps this explains why most FORTUNE 500 companies employ a chief communications officer. That person is responsible for advising the management team on appropriate messaging, behaviors, and perceptions. Successful CEOs know that communication is so critical to their ultimate success, that they put a professional on their team to advise them.

---

**EXAMPLE: The cost of poor communication**

Companies that fail to communicate lose money. A study of 400 large corporations found they lost an average $62.4 million a year due to poor communication. Smaller organizations lost an average of $420,000 a year.[32]

Failing to communicate turns out to be much more expensive than communicating well in the first place.

---

## Great communication: A thousand years in the making

Thinking about how to successfully craft and send a message is nothing new. One of the first communication coaches was Aristotle, and his advice on the topic is timeless. According to him, there are three elements of effective messaging: *Ethos, pathos,* and *logos*.

Ethos—the origin of our word *ethics*—is your credibility or character. It's the reason people should listen to you in the first place. When you communicate, do you possess the requisite technical skill or domain expertise on the topic? If you do, great—you've got permission from your audience to tell them what you think.

You need pathos too, which relates to emotions; it's the origin of our words *empathy* and *sympathy*. When you communicate, are you able to establish an emotional connection with your audience? Effective communicators accomplish this even in the leanest settings.

Finally, there's logos or *logic*—a focus on order and structure. Are your missives backed up by facts and figures? Does what you're saying make sense and come from a base of clear thought? That's necessary if you want to be effective.

Together, these three elements of Aristotle's framework reinforce themselves. Draw on them as you build your messages, and you will be in good stead.

In this chapter we're going to simplify and structure the process of communicating clearly. Whether you're meeting in person or online; talking to team members, customers, or other external stakeholders; you need to get your message across. Here we'll give you tools and insights for mastering this vital skill. Take the time to honestly assess how well you communicate in writing and in person. You will find that a few small changes will yield major dividends in this skill area.

## Chapter goals

Communication is an essential leadership skill—one that many leaders don't do well. That's in part because we need to keep a lot in mind whenever we're communicating.

When you're done here, you will be able to:

- Gain awareness of how effectively you currently communicate
- Evaluate and incorporate the needs and differences of your audience
- Simplify and structure your communications for maximum impact
- Craft robust messages that reach and resonate with your intended audience

---

**EXERCISE: Clear messaging—self-assessment**

Let's delve into this chapter by getting a sense of how clearly you currently communicate.

Rate yourself using the following scale:
0: Never, 1: Occasionally, 2: Often, 3: Always

| Clear messaging—self-assessment | | | | |
|---|---|---|---|---|
| I clarify the purpose of my communications. | 0 | 1 | 2 | 3 |
| I consider the needs of my audiences. | 0 | 1 | 2 | 3 |
| I craft messages that resonate with my audiences. | 0 | 1 | 2 | 3 |

## TWELVE SKILLS

| | | | | |
|---|---|---|---|---|
| I choose the right mediums for message distribution. | 0 | 1 | 2 | 3 |
| I convey messages in ways that provide maximum impact. | 0 | 1 | 2 | 3 |
| Total score | | | | |

If you scored 13 or greater, you're already a strong communicator. Well done. If you landed in the 8 to 12 range, you have an opportunity to make enhancements. If you rated yourself 7 or below, you'll want to incorporate the key points in this chapter in your communications.

Now that you know your strengths and weaknesses in communication, let's think about what communication really is and look at strategies for improvement you can put into practice right away.

## Clear messaging defined

What is clear messaging in business? Author Deborah Roebuck makes a distinction between managerial communication and leadership communication:

- **Managerial communication.** Communication within the organization between managers and employees that enables the organization's work.

- **Leadership communication.** Addresses both external and internal audiences, with a focus on leading change and inspiring with vision.[33]

Successful business leaders today, Roebuck posits, need to combine these aspects to excel at managerial leadership communication, or what we call *clear messaging*. These leaders deliver strong, effective communication that motivates team members and builds excitement for big-picture goals, inside and outside their organizations. Improving your ability to accomplish this is central to your success as a leader.

## Skill builder Four: 5C clear messaging process

At the highest level, it doesn't matter whether you are communicating in writing or verbally—the process is still the same.

We distill communication down into five steps:

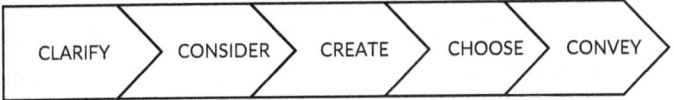

1. **Clarify:** Determine exactly why this message is being sent.

2. **Consider:** Evaluate the needs of the target audiences.

3. **Create:** Craft the message that will be sent, keeping in mind Aristotle's basic elements.

4. **Choose:** Select the best mediums in which to transmit the message.
5. **Convey:** Send the message to the intended audiences.

Now let's discuss each one in depth.

## Clarify

The first, often skipped step in communicating is clarifying what you are initially hoping to accomplish with your message. You might be saying to yourself, *Of course I know what I want my messages to do—that's why I'm putting them together in the first place.* However, by taking a step back and thinking through the range of outcomes your message may instigate, you will increase the chance that it will do exactly what you want.

For example, do you want your speech to provide information? In that case, be sure you mention all of the pertinent details, along with covering questions people are likely to have. Draw on your credibility or *ethos* in this case.

Are you trying to persuade people to adopt a point of view? You need to present a compelling argument if you are. Think *logos*.

Is the purpose of your email to get people to act? If it is, you want to be sure they understand what they need to do and that your message appeals to their sensibilities, along with including particulars on how those people can act successfully. Here's where *pathos* features strongly. Working through this step will help ensure you connect with your audience.

In her chapter on developing written communication skills, author Roebuck lists these basic objectives in communicating:

- Seek ideas or facts
- Send ideas or facts
- Inspire an action (buy a product, get on our mailing list)
- Educate or instruct
- Persuade
- Promote goodwill[34]

Once you've clarified your purpose, then you'll want to be sure you put yourself in the mind of the reader or listener.

## Consider

The next step is to consider the needs of those receiving your message. Carefully think about the answers to a few questions to frame your message properly:

- How do you think they'll react?
- What is their frame of mind?

- What is their familiarity with the topic or their level of sophistication?
- Will they be amenable to your message or is there fear—or worse, hostility—in the background?

Thinking about audiences' information needs and emotional state will aid in the development of messages that resonate with them. You can then decide if your message should be formal or informal, short or more detailed. For example, your word choices for an audience of PhD biochemists would be different from if you were speaking to a group of hourly wage workers at a manufacturing facility.

Whatever your audience, resist the urge to use complex words and, if possible, try to avoid using highly technical terms or acronyms. Simplicity and clarity will foster greater understanding and engagement.

Another consideration is whether you want to be direct or indirect. If you have good news or a pleasant announcement to make, you can take a direct approach. Like a journalist writing a news story, you can get right to core bits of the message, leading with the most important information up front. Many people don't read long messages, and they lose interest in lengthy presentations. Putting the bottom line up front is a way to ensure your key points are received.

On the other hand, if you need to share bad news, or if you worry your communication will trigger negative emotions or perhaps not attract interest, you might choose an indirect approach. You begin with a neutral or positive soft statement that puts the reader in a receptive frame of mind. After that, you deliver the difficult part of the communication and then end with another positive sentiment or statement.

With all these techniques, you can see how important it is to know your audience so you know how to structure your message.

## Create

Once you've clarified your purpose and considered your audience, it's time to create the message you want to deliver. Keep in mind: Your message is where you will present your ideas. To make sure your message succeeds, it should arrive in a form your audience understands.

Often it's best to write a quick first draft; an outline works well for both a written piece and a verbal presentation. On the first pass, try not to self-censor or start editing; get the content out into a rough format for the purpose of capturing your initial ideas. From the Clarify section, there are three basic types of messages: They inform, persuade, or prompt action, or any combination of these. If you try to do all three at once, your audience may be overwhelmed, so be sure to break up your message and deliver it in several pieces, rather than trying to do everything in one go.

Another consideration is how this message will make recipients feel. If you're expecting intense emotions, slow down. Managerial leaders get out in front of recipients' emotions by acknowledging them and then prescribing a way forward. Say something like: "I understand this may make you feel [emotion]. Here's what I recommend…"

Then the real work comes: Creating the final written work or presentation. Even professionals don't create amazing works on their first draft, so don't skimp on time here. A few tips to keep in mind:

- **The opening elements are all-important.** Make sure first pages or slides fascinate.

- **Eliminate verbiage.** If you can say the same thing in fewer words, do it.

- **Review transitions.** Does each thought logically lead to the next, whether between paragraphs or PowerPoint slides? If not, reorganize.

- **End strongly.** What is the takeaway or the action you want the recipients to take? Try to narrow your conclusion down to a single thought or request.

Before you declare victory on your message, be sure you've proofed and polished your draft. If it's a written piece, proofread for small mistakes. Nothing undermines your message like a typo that makes your communication seem half-baked. For example, a software tool such as Grammarly helps as you are creating; and the Read Aloud function in Word is excellent at catching misspelled, missing, and misused words. In the case of presentations, do the same, but have someone watch a dry run of your delivery, listening for points that might be unclear, or which might miss what the audience will be listening for. Also, make it a point to find and remove repetitive words and phrases, jargon, and overly complex concepts or sentences.

If you have time, it's a good idea to put your work away for a day and then revisit your final draft. A fresh set of eyes will help refine your message before you press send.

## Choose

Once your intended message is created, it's time to decide how to deliver it. As you know, there's a wide range of communication channels. The table below provides a summary based on the richness and effort of each channel.

## Communication Channels

| Rich channel<br>(high impact / high effort) | Lean channel<br>(low impact / low effort) |
|---|---|
| Face to face<br><br>Video conferencing<br><br>Telephone | Addressed written documents (for example, letters, emails, instant messages, text)<br><br>Unaddressed written documents (for example, reports, bulletins)<br><br>Bulk mail<br><br>Posters, fliers |

It's important that you choose the right channel for the audience, depending on the importance of the message and the cost and effort of the communication. You don't want to end up like the wrong-headed CEO who was widely denounced as heartless after firing 900 employees shortly before Christmas during a group Zoom call.[35] Choosing the wrong delivery channel can damage your reputation.

Early in our careers, both of us worked in companies during mergers and/or acquisitions. It's hard to imagine an employee today who hasn't experienced the same. Often during initial announcements, top leaders gather employees and personally deliver messages regarding the reasoning and impact of the transaction. Because of the sensitivity of the messages, in-person meetings or video conferencing are often preferable. However, as the mergers unfold

## DEVELOPING CLEAR MESSAGING

over time, and managers work on the details of implementation, email and other forms of mass communication may be the most effective mediums. Your choice will depend again on the purpose of the communication and the outcome you wish to achieve.

One technique we recommend: Don't rely on only one channel of communication. People learn differently, and many learn in stages. For example, you might deliver your message first in a group meeting and then follow up with one-to-one meetings with each team member, or with an email. This approach allows you to gauge how each audience and—in some cases—each individual reacts to the message. It also helps in gathering feedback.

Remember that some people learn better by reading, others by listening, still others by writing points down. Many of us need more than one method to retain new information. Consider, for example, following up a Zoom call with an email. Whatever methods you choose, be deliberate in your approach and mindful of differences in your team members.

Don't forget that, with increased workplace diversity, reactions will vary greatly. A younger team member may view you as a mentor they'd never challenge. Others may have lived experiences similar to that of your target customer and could be recruited as project leaders. Some people may immediately grasp what you're saying, while others are distracted by your tone of voice, or because they are thinking about a personal matter. Always be mindful of your audience and select your medium accordingly.

## Convey

If you've followed all the steps to this point, you're ready to deliver your message. If it's a written communication, your job at this point might be simply hitting send on your email or dropping your letter into a mailbox. If you're delivering your presentation verbally, you'll want to consider a few additional steps.

### *Prepare*

Organize your presentation into a logical sequence, ensuring your slides and messages are tailored to your audience and their interests. Remember that shorter is always better. If you present too many concepts, the audience won't remember them all. Author Roebuck recommends using the *rule of three*—likely the maximum number of points your audience will retain.

Use your outline to create your speaker's notes or the script you'll take to the podium. As your speech date nears, gather the support material you need—any famous quotes, analogies, statistics, illustrations, and the like.

## DEVELOPING CLEAR MESSAGING

**PREPARATION TIP**

Prepare your outline before your visual aids to avoid wasting time designing unneeded presentation slides or video clips.

Visuals greatly help listeners to receive and retain your message, but only if they're simple and graphical rather than a copy of your spoken points.

Think big, bold, beautiful images.

---

Finally, think ahead about Q&As so you can formulate answers to likely questions in advance. This will help reduce presentation anxiety. If there are questions you know people will have, feel free to plant someone in the audience who is willing to ask the question if it isn't raised by anyone else.

## *Practice*

The more anxious you are about public speaking, the more time you should spend practicing. Practice helps ease fears and build confidence. You may be surprised to learn that public speaking didn't come naturally to British Prime Minister Winston Churchill. He never tried to memorize his speeches and famously spent days practicing before delivering an address.

Ideally, plan short practice sessions, spread across several days. Research has shown this helps cement the speech in your mind better than a single, long practice session. As you practice, look for opportunities to refine your message. A sentence may appear articulate on paper but prove too convoluted when spoken, for instance. Take a cue from TV news: Short, punchy words and sentences are easiest for ears to parse.

Usually, listeners don't have a written copy of your speech. Use the classic classroom-teaching structure to reinforce your points: Tell them what they'll learn, present your ideas, then recap what they have learned. Setup, delivery, recap is a time-tested way to make your messages stick.

## PRACTICE TIPS

- Pay attention to tone and body language. If you say it's good news but you never smile, the audience may doubt you.
- Practice the toughest likely questions for Q&A time.
- Record yourself so you can review and improve.
- Remember to pause for breath. Pausing is important, both to make sure you keep breathing, and for the audience members, who need breaks to digest your ideas.
- Cut filler words such as *um* or *OK*.
- Consider adding more visual cues to your presentation to break up text.
- Do a dress rehearsal in the clothes and makeup you'll wear for the presentation.

When you review your practice recording or get peer feedback, ask yourself if you, as an audience member, would pay attention to your presentation. If not, keep tweaking until it is more compelling.

## Present

You've prepped and practiced, and now you're ready to deliver your speech. Kinds of items that will help you feel fully prepared include your notes, a slide advancer, a pointer, batteries for the advancer and microphone, and a bottle of water. Another way to gain confidence is by showing up early to the presentation location and getting yourself completely set up. Also, do a sound check, to make sure everyone can hear you.

## PRESENTATION TIPS

- Use gestures to emphasize key points.
- Make eye contact around the room.
- Dress one level up from the audience for a strong first impression.
- Go off-script, adding an anecdote or story.
- Make eye contact and smile—it'll relax you and your audience.
- Let the audience know when you'll take questions.
- Watch your tone of voice and delivery speed.
- If you have a podium, feel free to walk in an arc near it and then return.
- Make your audience feel valued. If you don't know the answer to a question, let them know you'll research and report back.

If you're presenting as part of a team, it adds to the complexity of mastering your delivery. You need to prepare and practice *with* your team, to make sure you coordinate well. Define roles in advance and be clear on timing for each person. There's nothing worse than a group of people standing in front of the room looking at each other with confused faces while the audience waits for something to happen.

For important messages you'll deliver to a small group or one on one, you may also want to do a similar but less intense preparation process.

---

Given the pervasive use of blog posts, social media, and texting, we have included our thoughts on these emerging communication media.

## *Blog posts*

Blogging can be a powerful way to quickly get ideas across. A growing number of executives either guest post on popular blogs or publish their own blog. Blog posts can burnish your authority, help you stand out at your organization, and build your audience. What makes a good blog post? A few quick tips:

- **The headline is 80% of the post.** Think about what searches people would do for your topic (ideally, grab a free SEO tool and research phrases). Then write a fresh, interesting headline that includes a search phrase. Use emotion words to drive interest, for example, *shocking, surprising, heartbreaking.*

- **Deliver on your headline's promise.** Keep a tight focus and prune any side trails.

- **Link to useful resources.** Posts should have at least one external link to an authoritative source, and one to another useful post on the same site.

- **Write for skimmers.** Most blog readers don't read every word.[36] Use subheadings or bulleted/numbered lists so readers get the gist even if they quickly scan through your blog.

- **Respond to comments.** A good blog post starts a conversation.

*Social media*

Social media may be the biggest communication minefield executives face today. One update that hits people wrong can get you fired.[37] On the other hand, experts can strengthen their reputations and expand their reach in social channels. Many books have been written on social media best practices; we have a few overarching tips for you:

**SOCIAL MEDIA TIPS**

- They call it social media because people primarily want to socialize. It's a great place to humanize yourself. Share your journey—a slice of life from a good or bad day. Don't sell.

- Many people dish out smack talk on social media, criticizing or calling out others' mistakes. All we can say is: Think before you tweet. Kindness is free.
- Once you post on social media, it belongs to the world forever. Even if you later delete it, others may have taken screenshots or can find a copy in internet archives... it never goes away.
- With any social channel, watch and learn first. See who is popular and what sort of posts seem to get a lot of response, then craft your message.
- With the rise of Instagram and Pinterest, all social channels have become increasingly visual. Studies show pictures attract interest and are easier to understand than text.[38] Consider whether a captioned picture could be more impactful than a long missive.

---

### *Texting*

SMS is the new marketing frontier, and an increasingly common way executives communicate. Nobody wants to read "The Gettysburg Address" on their phone—keep texts short.

Two key things to know about texts: They're not private, and you don't own them. The recipient owns their copy, and your phone carrier may save one too. As American political commentator Tucker Carlson found out, private text messages sent between work colleagues aren't private at all. What he wrote cost him his job, and Fox News $757 million dollars.[39]

Text like the world is watching. It's easy for one colleague to send your text to another colleague.

> **TEXTING TIP**
>
> Don't text if you're feeling emotional. You can be fired for inappropriate text messages you've sent.[40] Never continue texting someone who has asked you to stop.
>
> Of all written forms, texting seems to be the hardest for reading tone. It's easy to be misunderstood, so type carefully.

## Getting started with effective messaging

In this chapter you learned the 5C clear messaging process: Clarify, Consider, Create, Choose, and Convey. Within these you reviewed ideas and tips you can put to work right away to shore up how you craft and send messages.

That said, below are thoughts to get you off on the right path:

- **Keep differences in mind.** People have different genders, ages, backgrounds, life experiences, and cultural histories. Remember different audiences may need different messages and different mediums to reach them effectively.

- **Check for confusion.** Many words, idioms, and examples have multiple meanings, opening the door to possible misunderstandings. Be sensitive to how messages might get jumbled up in someone's eyes or ears.

- **Avoid information overload.** We're confronted with more information than any previous generation. Avoid potential overload and *bottom-line* your message—keep it simple and to the point.

Messaging may be both the simplest and most difficult skill you will learn about in this book. Never stop seeking feedback on how you can improve. Brilliant communication is a fast-track ticket to advancement. Every organization needs leaders who can clearly describe goals, build relationships with team members, and motivate employees to get things done.

Your communication skills will be invaluable as you add the next skill. Clear messaging will help you create strong relationships at your workplace.

# 5
# Expanding Relationship Building

Leaders need to inspire others and guide their teams toward their goals. To do that, they need to get people to buy into their plans and work together. How do leaders get people to do what they want them to do? By building relationships.

Think for a moment: We spend nearly a third of our lives at work. Our work lives will be an absolute chore if we find that work time unfulfilling. In contrast, the sense of accomplishment, pride, and fellowship when you have a sense of camaraderie and community at work is virtually unbounded. For many people, their deepest purpose is found inside their relationships with the people they work with.

## Why relationship building?

In his article 'The Power of Work Friends', Jon Clifton, CEO of Gallup, describes how having friends at work—specifically, a best friend—improves business outcomes, profitability, and retention as well as other key metrics.[41] Further, people experience a heightened sense of loyalty when they have friends at work, even if they're in completely different parts of the organization.

None of us want to let our friends down, especially when those friends are there for us when we need them. Good leaders don't only foster relationships between themselves and colleagues—they also seek to build relationships among their team members and in the organization overall. Invest your time to create an environment in which meaningful relationships can thrive for your team members; they'll feel valued, and you'll engender loyalty. Don't stop there—it's just as important to invest time in establishing meaningful relationships for yourself.

## Chapter goals

You've likely been building relationships your whole life. After this chapter, you'll be more aware of everyone's emotions, including your own. You will also have a sense of what you need to do to grow and harvest value from your network.

# EXPANDING RELATIONSHIP BUILDING

When you're done reading this chapter, you will be able to:

- Understand what Emotional Intelligence (EI) is and how it impacts relationship building
- Learn techniques to start new relationships, and expand and strengthen existing ones
- Discover ways to build and manage your professional network

---

**EXERCISE: Expanding relationships—self-assessment**

There's no doubt you're already managing workplace relationships. To identify where you can make improvements, let's get a better sense of where your strengths and opportunities are.

Rate yourself using the following scale:
0: Never, 1: Occasionally, 2: Often, 3: Always

| Relationships—self-assessment | | | | |
|---|---|---|---|---|
| I have high emotional intelligence. | 0 | 1 | 2 | 3 |
| I engage regularly with new people as well as in my most important relationships. | 0 | 1 | 2 | 3 |
| I am focused on expanding my network. | 0 | 1 | 2 | 3 |
| Total score | | | | |

A score of 7 or more, and you likely have solid, productive relationships. If you landed in 5 or 6 territory, opportunities await you. If you rated yourself 4 or below, you have ample upside in relationship building. By the time you are finished applying this skill, you should have a solid set of growing relationships on hand.

## Relationship building defined

Relationships are the nature of the connections we have with other people. We typically define them in terms of their strength or goodness. Too often we take our relationships for granted. It's a shame when we do, because they are an essential ingredient to our professional success. Why? It's simple—we depend on other people to get things done. It's common for professionals as they grow in their career to continue to act alone—like an army of one. *It's easier if I just do it myself* is a common phrase people too busy to delegate will say. If you want to succeed as a leader, you need to leverage your relationships. If you do not have strong relationships in place, you'll have difficulty moving up the corporate ladder.

Linda Hill, professor of business administration at Harvard Business School, looks at relationships from four angles:

1. People whose cooperation you need

2. People whose compliance you need

3. People who oppose you

4. People who need your cooperation and compliance[42]

This is a useful way to think about interdependencies in the workplace. As you work your way through this chapter, think about the relationships you have at work through the lens of Professor Hill's four dimensions.

## Skill builder Five: 3E relationship-building process

Can something as complex as a relationship be boiled down to a simple set of steps? In short, yes. Our three-step relationship process will create the awareness and start you on the actions you need to cultivate purposeful connections at work.

The relationship-building steps are:

1. **Express:** Be aware of and regulate your emotions; be sensitive to the emotions of those around you.

2. **Engage:** Keep growing your circle of influence, regularly assess your network, add strategic contacts and remove ineffective ones.

3. **Expand:** Take steps to build new connections and keep existing work connections vibrant.

Now that you've taken stock of your current relationship-building skills, let's break down each of our three steps to better understand relationships in detail. We'll begin with a key relationship-building skill that many leaders aren't attuned to: Understanding and expressing emotional intelligence.

## Express

Have you ever worked with someone who says or does things that rub others the wrong way? For example, they say something inappropriate about a colleague's appearance or someone else's presentation. In a meeting, a mid-level colleague once started criticizing the founder of our company in front of all the other employees. While the founder handled the disparaging comments well, everyone in the room felt the tension and awkwardness. The person making the comments felt justified and seemed unfazed by the situation. This is a case where we might remark to ourselves, *That person has no self-awareness.* Behaviors like this—and many others—are often associated with someone having low emotional intelligence.

What is emotional intelligence? In his article, "What Makes a Leader?", Daniel Goleman, one of the forefathers of the emotional intelligence concept, notes EI comprises five components:

- Self-awareness: Knowing your strengths, weaknesses, values, and motivations and their effect on others

- Self-regulation: Your ability to control disruptive emotions or impulses

- Motivation: Your drive to achieve for the sake of it

- Empathy: The degree to which you consider others feelings, especially when making decisions

- Social skill: How you manage social relationships[43]

### *Self-awareness, self-regulation, and social skill*

Think about self-awareness, self-regulation, and social skill—three components of emotional intelligence that may be the most essential for relationships. For instance, you may not think anything of eating at your desk, but the rest of your team or colleagues may feel you're avoiding them when you don't sit with them at lunch. Similarly, if you're having a bad day from a flat tire or spilling coffee on your clothes, venting your frustration on your colleagues (or on the café barista) is a sign that your self-regulation is low.

Think about whether you've ever done something like that—expressing your anger on a colleague. You might think, *Well, I was just frustrated—it's normal to feel and act that way. Heck, I just spilled hot coffee all over myself, of course I'm upset!* Feeling that way is normal. Recognizing it shows strong self-awareness. Acting out based on that kind of frustration is a sign of poor self-regulation and low social skill. This kind of behavior impairs the functioning of relationships. While it might not seem a big deal to you, it will to others, who may start viewing you as hot-headed and to be avoided.

As a baseline: You need to be well regulated emotionally and aware of how you're perceived. A leader who creates an environment where people feel nervous or uncomfortable has little chance of fostering relationships. To the contrary, they may even be in danger of creating a hostile workplace.

### *Empathy and motivation*

Two other facets of emotional intelligence are key for forming engaging relationships: Empathy and motivation. Psychologist Goleman defines empathy as "considering others' feelings, especially when making decisions."

Empathy enables leaders to attract, develop, and retain key talent. You can hardly build a constructive, functional work relationship with colleagues if you're oblivious to their emotional needs and reactions to your behavior. Moreover, empathy and understanding are of increasing importance in a workplace that is growing increasingly diverse. Only increased empathy—taking the time to listen to and understand other people's concerns—will help leaders serve a global, diverse, and inclusive market.

Motivation is your drive to achieve. It's why you're reading this book right now. You want to get ahead and excel in your career, meaning you have the individual motivation to achieve success, however you define it. You also need motivation to follow the steps we highlight in building your relationships. An ounce of motivation is worth at least a pound of education.

With emotional intelligence defined, the obvious question is, *Can I improve mine?* The answer is a resounding *yes*. The secret is motivation. You have to want it. If you're motivated to build this skill, practice and feedback are key. You want mentors who can tell you whether your remarks show empathy to your team, and if you are aware of your own emotions and how your team is connecting. Ask your team members for their feedback, and remember: You need to thank them for their feedback and respond to it as well. Keep practicing, keep soliciting feedback, and keep improving. Lasting change always takes time, so if you want to grow your EI quotient, get started now and be patient and persistent. Make strides in this area, and you'll find improved emotional intelligence can be contagious—it will be good for both you and your team.

With your emotional intelligence on the upswing, you will be ready to use it to invigorate your relationships. You want to build authentic, vibrant, enduring relationships, and that's the next step in our model.

## Engage

We need to build and maintain engaging relationships with long-term colleagues as well as employees or partners we've just met. We need to be comfortable seeking new relationships, and we have to take steps to invest in those we already have—even with people we've known for a long time. People join and leave organizations, and individual circumstances change, as do personal needs. Relationships are always evolving. Given the importance of relationships to both success and satisfaction, we have to take steps to engage and increase their value.

### *New relationships*

Let's start with new relationships. When you're meeting someone for the first time—whether that's a new customer or a whole new set of work colleagues—it can be easy to hang back and simply go through the traditional motions. The obligatory handshake, monotone presentation of name and role—you know how it goes. For many people, creating new relationships, especially at work, is a major stressor. They see it as a problem rather than a terrific opportunity to cement their value and become more effective.

Resist the temptation to underrate a new introduction—make the most of your new connection. One of the best times to get started on building strong relationships is when you're meeting someone for the first time.

If you're hesitant to dive into relationship building, what's the solution? Keith Rollag, a Babson College management professor, suggests mastering three getting-to-know-you skills that will help you succeed in new situations.

- **Introduce yourself.** Don't be the kind of person who—like most people—only talks to people they know. Take the initiative to meet new people—especially more senior leaders. Practice your opening lines and, when conversing, really make it a point to listen. Put yourself in their shoes so you can see the conversation in a different light.

- **Remember names.** How many times have you heard someone say, "I'm sorry, I'm bad with names? Who are you again?" The way to avoid being that person is by not relying on your memory. As soon as you can after meeting someone, create a note about them, including key personal details (married, single, trains show dogs, competes in triathlons), along with any likes or dislikes you discovered. Use an image (for example, she had cool blue glasses) to create a jogger that will help you recall who they are. Be sure to review your notes when you're going to see people you haven't seen in a while, to refresh particulars about them.

- **Ask questions.** Remember, everyone's favorite radio station is KIAM—*Keep It About Me*—because most of us really enjoy listening to ourselves. Your questions and genuine listening show you're not just a good listener, but someone who is interested in others. Keep your questions short and to the point and follow up on what your conversationalist is telling you. Nothing will make you seem more interesting than sincerely paying attention to someone when they are talking to you.[44]

If you can make a solid first contact, you immediately begin to identify shared experiences and build rapport. That's how you expand your relationships.

## Existing relationships

What about existing relationships? If you already have good work relationships, don't take them for granted. Engaging relationships need to be nurtured to keep them strong. Especially if you've been in the same role a long time, it can feel awkward to suddenly start relationship-building with colleagues or your direct reports, but remember that even a small, subtle change can have a major impact.

In his article, "5 Steps to Building Great Business Relationships", veteran CEO and entrepreneur Jim Doherty, who teaches strategic management at MIT, identifies the keys to enhancing your business relationships:

- **Be likable.** Show people you're friendly, helpful, and interested in them. If you only talk about the fastest way to close the quarterly books, your likability doesn't shine through. Consider it an investment in your career to spend a few minutes each week discussing weekend plans, or asking about people, their pets, kids, or parents.

- **Be professionally respectable.** Competence and reliability matter a lot when it comes to building relationships at work. When your colleagues can rely on your skill and your ability to follow through, you become a valued resource and someone others will respect and seek out.

- **Be an admirable, whole person.** You are more than a supervisor, communications professional, or supply-chain manager. You are also a parent, sibling, child, volunteer, mountain climber or—dare I say—Marine reservist (like Ed) or competitive swimmer and Special Olympics swim coach (like Laura). As relationships evolve, a coworker may really want to know how your daughter's recital went, or if you won your adult-league soccer game.

- **Mingle lives.** In time, you may find opportunities to socialize outside of the office with people you work with. You may not be able to connect in the office, but somehow, you make a champion table tennis, trivia, or skee-ball team player at the local bar. Sharing a meal and laughing together goes far.

- **Maintain contact after a business relationship is no longer necessary.** If a relationship is real, it will transcend the workplace and last the test of time. When you change jobs, keep the connections you've made. Holiday cards are good, but periodic calls are better. Touch base to discuss a work challenge they have, or an idea you had that might help them. Let them know you haven't stopped caring.[45]

We know one writer who helped her publications editors by sending them job leads after they were laid off. They may not have got those jobs, but you can bet when they did secure a new position, they called her up with assignments. As those editors moved into different roles over time, she ended up adding several new publications as clients.

Whatever the current state of your relationships, you can always use Doherty's five principles to improve them. Once you've fully engaged with your new and existing relationships, you can move on to the final step: Expanding your network.

### Expand

It's easy to get stuck in a relationship rut, relying on existing connections you built long ago, but savvy leaders are constantly growing their circle of influence. This requires thoughtfully building your network. In fact, it's one of the most important things you can do

## EXPANDING RELATIONSHIP BUILDING

to advance in your career. Don't panic—we're not suggesting you print a new set of business cards and sign up for a dozen networking groups. Ours is a more strategic and more enjoyable approach.

What exactly *is* a network, anyway? It's a collection of people who exchange information and connections as well as offering professional advice and support. In business, you're only as strong as who and what you know, the resources you can access, and what you've accomplished. Right? Well, not exactly. In the professional realm, you're judged not just for what you know, accomplish, and experience, but also for the cumulative knowledge, resources, and information you can *access through your network*. That's a critical point. A leader who can access different parts of their own organizations and their own ecosystem is infinitely more valuable than someone who can't. That's why networking is so crucial to success as a leader.

You can't occupy several different roles or work in different industries at the same time, but you can expand your outlook through relationships with people in many roles and industries. A diverse network means you know more, giving you unique insights that help build your credibility and authority. The power unleashed by this broader knowledge base can be astonishing.

**TWELVE SKILLS**

---

**EXAMPLE: Network power**

Joe [not his real name] was a successful real estate developer who contributed his time, talent, and treasure to several different organizations. He was particularly passionate about finding solutions for opioid addiction. At one point, he was invited to the White House to address an influential committee that was considering measures to fight the epidemic. Over time, he had become one of the most knowledgeable people in the country on the topic. Rather than immediately catching the DC shuttle, though, Joe first quickly convened an online gathering of a dozen or so other experts based around the globe. He solicited their thoughts, some of which differed from his own.

In DC he presented not only his ideas but also the consensus views of his peers. Thanks to his network's insights, he was able to share divergent perspectives. His influence profile seemed higher because he consulted other experts, and his recommendations were taken more seriously.

---

Maybe you don't travel in these sorts of high-powered circles—yet—but you can if you build the right network. Remember, great connections can come from anywhere: Your college roommate may be a CEO one day, or your neighbor may want to hire you to lead her North American division. One of us worked with two colleagues during a summer internship, and they now hold senior-level roles—one is the CEO of a major insurance carrier; the other is a senior vice president of a major technology company responsible for worldwide smartphone sales. Bottom line: The more strategic and planned your network is, the more of an advantage it is to you.

## How to start building

How do you build your network? It starts with the people around you—friends and colleagues. Usually, you share common interests—say, indoor rock climbing, a topical book club, or the same workplace. Over time, your connections grow through an exchange of ideas, or through assistance such as introductions or referrals. Remember, you're not building a circle of friends—you're building a professional network. That means you need to connect with people who can help you advance your professional interests.

Always be on the lookout for valuable connections. When a friend from the gym asks you to review their resume, do it. If you see an article about high-growth companies expanding into South America, you can forward it to your friend in the São Paulo office. When you're looking for a better job, one of those people may know the perfect opportunity, but if you haven't connected with them in three years, you may be reluctant to reach out. As we discussed in the second step: Keep your relationships fresh.

Those of you who work in sales or professional service roles may do these things already. For example, you may be in the habit of scheduling a professional breakfast a few times a month, writing notecards to thank people for meeting with you, or hopping on video conferences just to say "Hi." Leaders with command of this skill do too.

Remember, the point is to keep connecting with people who can help you in your career, so you always need to seek the right people to reach out to. Be generous to your new connections. Look for ways to help them and show them you can deliver value first and foremost. The more strategic your network, the better. You may not know how you could help someone or how someone might help you right now, but when you're connected to the right people, eventually a way to create value will present itself.

*Evaluating your network*

Here's something they don't teach you in business school: A network doesn't only expand—sometimes it needs to be pared back. Some people are no longer active members of your professional network, though they may still be connections. That's why it's important to periodically evaluate and prune your network on, say, an annual basis. It's important to ask yourself how recently you interacted with your contacts. Does each contact add to the diversity of your network, or is it someone much like yourself in their outlook, career stage, and opinions? If not, removal may be in order.

To systematize the evaluation process, try this: Make a chart with columns to evaluate the health of your network. (You can find a great example created by Brian Uzzi, leadership professor at Northwestern's Kellogg School of Management.) Begin by listing your top twenty-five professional contacts. Note these factors about each:

- Are they internal or external (from your workplace or elsewhere)?
- Are they similar to or different from you?
- Who introduced you to this person?
- Who have they connected you with?
- Who have you connected them with?
- What do you see as the value of the connection?
- How strong is this connection?

The above list is by no means exhaustive, but you get the idea—create questions that help you see both the quality of each individual connection and the patterns to the types of people in your network. Doing so should help you:

- **Discover types of people to add.** Identify types of people who would add diversity. Perhaps you need more people in other industries, or younger execs with fresh insights. Also think about ethnic and cultural diversity, and reach out to people with different lived experiences.

- **Find super-connectors to nurture.** Are there any connections who have introduced you to many other people? Anyone who has introduced you to your most important contacts? These super-connectors are invaluable—think about ways to retain and nurture them.

- **Identify obsolete connections.** Did you list people who, on reflection, are people with whom you don't share connections, information, or support? These people aren't really part of your network, so think about who could replace them.

Use your chart to help you prioritize your outreach activities. Your network should grow ever more diverse and valuable as you build relationships. Think if it as an asset—one that will help you get where you want to go in your career.

## Getting started with relationship building

The 3E relationship-building process of Express, Engage, and Expand will help you improve your existing relationships and accelerate the development of new ones. The success of virtually every organization is based on its people, which makes fostering strong relationships a key ingredient of a leader's success.

To strengthen your relationships, here are things you can do right away:

- **Reframe relationships.** Make the relationships you have with your team members and your colleagues central to your leadership agenda. Invest the kind of time in them that you would invest in any strategic project.

- **Go one on one.** Every person is different, which makes every relationship different. Recognize the need to build personal relationships with your colleagues so you can create the kinds of bonds that make a meaningful difference.

- **Share the wealth.** Don't make it purely your personal mission to develop strong relationships—encourage the people around you to do the same.

Our next skill relies on the strength of your relationship-building abilities. As you grow relationships, you will probably identify people you think have management potential. They could benefit from professional development, and as a leader, it's your job to create that pathway.

# 6
# Strengthening Talent Development

It's never been easier for talented executives, directors, or frontline staff to send a resignation email to their boss and decamp for better pay, a better working environment, and greater upward mobility. In short, the nature of business and society today has inspired many people to reevaluate how, where, and even whether they want to work. The result? People are changing jobs, changing careers, and leaving the workforce completely for gig work or even no work. This places an enormous burden on employers to retain their talent.

Employees want to feel they're compensated fairly, respected, and have opportunities for development and advancement. As a leader, a major component of your job—no matter at what level you are—is to develop your team's skills and let them know they're valued. In this chapter we'll give you practical strategies you can use to win the talent war on three fronts: Through better hiring, improved retention, and enhanced development, as you put your employees on a clear promotion path for future opportunity.

## Why talent development?

Think there aren't rewards in developing talent? Think again. In a 2017 study of over 14,500 workers, researchers Zorana Ivcevic, Robin Stern, and Andrew Faas found that 85% reported they aren't working at 100% of their potential.[46] Of those, 16% said they aren't even using 50% of their potential at their current job. The bottom line is that environmental and workplace changes have paired a new premium and opportunity on talent development—one that is more important than ever before and, in some cases, more challenging too. The success of the modern organization depends on leaders' abilities in finding and developing talent. That's why it's one of the Twelve Skills.

## Chapter goals

By the end of this chapter, you will have a better handle on how to hire and develop talent. Keep in mind: Your team members will be key drivers of your success as a leader, so you want them to be top-tier players.

# STRENGTHENING TALENT DEVELOPMENT

When you've finished this chapter, you will be able to:

- Attract the talent you need for key positions
- Provide constructive feedback and coaching to employees on their development journey
- Continually manage performance using a straightforward process

---

**EXERCISE: Talent development—self-assessment**

If you have people that work for you, or even with you, how well do you think you currently develop them? What time and energy do you commit to building the skills of those you work with? Take a few minutes to reflect and think about the extent to which you are both a talent magnet and talent builder.

Rate yourself using the following scale:
0: Never, 1: Occasionally, 2: Often, 3: Always

| Talent development—self-assessment | | | | |
|---|---|---|---|---|
| I try to attract (identify, screen, and hire) a diverse mix of candidates that reflect our organization's values and culture. | 0 | 1 | 2 | 3 |
| I make it a point to develop both the technical and leadership skills of my team and colleagues. | 0 | 1 | 2 | 3 |
| I spend a significant amount of my time coaching my team members by observing them and providing feedback, to improve their performance and retain them in the business. | 0 | 1 | 2 | 3 |

**TWELVE SKILLS**

| I utilize a formal or informal performance management process to guide talent development overall. | 0 | 1 | 2 | 3 |
|---|---|---|---|---|
| Total score | | | | |

This is a skill that is often overlooked by leaders, so if you gave yourself a score of 9 or more, you're doing a noteworthy job developing your team. If you rated yourself from 6 to 8, you can make a greater impact with your team's development. If you were 5 or under, you're missing out on the opportunity to be a leader that builds those around you. If you work through this chapter and make a commitment to the practices herein, you'll start seeing a measurable improvement in the capabilities of those around you, and likely in your unit's performance too.

## Talent development defined

Talent development is a term that's so broad, it's apt to convey little value—almost anything related to managing people can be tucked somewhere under the umbrella phrase. Peter Cappelli of the Wharton School notes in his article "Talent Management for the Twenty-First Century": "Talent management is simply a matter of anticipating the need for human capital and then setting out a plan to meet it."[47]

This is helpful in terms of getting closer to a working definition, but still—for a leader to be effective when it comes to developing people, there must be a clearer set of steps. The Harvard Business Publishing Corporate Learning blog lists three key steps that comprise what we call the talent development cycle: Attracting, developing, and retaining employees. That's a straightforward definition, but moving from theory to practice is more challenging. Our model will help smooth the process.

## Skill builder Six: HDCM talent development process

Our experience over the years is consistent with the talent management definitions we provide.

There are four important steps that constitute the talent development process in which leaders need to be actively engaged, regardless of their level in an organization:

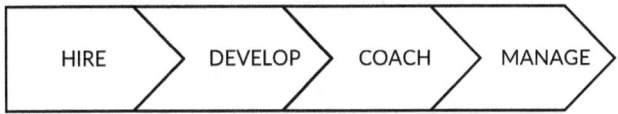

1. **Hire:** Engage in the process, carefully craft job descriptions, and conduct bias-free interviews.

2. **Develop:** Onboard new hires and provide opportunities for technical and leadership-skills development for all employees.

3. **Coach:** Guide employees, give feedback and offer constructive suggestions; coach them on how to find solutions on their own.

4. **Manage:** Use a continuous performance management cycle to help your team improve.

It's likely that you've participated in—or managed—these steps at some point in your working career. They shouldn't be foreign to you. What might be a little different is viewing them not as independent steps but as part of an ongoing process of talent development.

Pulling the distinct activities together is where the power of talent development comes to life. Let's explore the process from start to finish.

## Hire

It's hard to develop future leaders if you don't hire the right people. To build a stellar team that supports your goals, you need to identify outstanding candidates, but how do you pull that off? The best way to ensure you hire great employees is first and foremost to engage in the hiring process.

### *Engage in the hiring process*

It's no secret that leaders who excel at talent development start at the beginning by taking an active role in the hiring process. While the human resources team may help inform the process and source candidates, they don't fully understand the skills and personal qualities needed. That's your job as the hiring manager; after all, the new recruits will be working for you. Consider recruiting as an ongoing part of your job. Constantly build your network and look for people you think the organization should hire—and people who *know* people you should hire. When it's time to hire, you'll be one step ahead, with strong candidates you can invite to apply for a position.

How can you tell if a candidate will be a good fit for the organization? As simple as it sounds, it all begins with a good job description.

### *Write an effective job description*

Many organizations hire people who aren't suited to their role, due to poorly crafted job descriptions. Too often, leaders simply recycle old descriptions, or let HR write them, when the leaders themselves best understand the requirements. Here are some points to consider in creating job descriptions, from the Harvard Business School Press report, "Hiring Process: Attracting the Best People":

- **Define primary responsibilities.** List what the departing person actually did in their role (or if a brand-new role, what the requirements will be). Should the new hire take on the same responsibilities? This is a chance to reimagine this role. Are some tasks obsolete or better taken on by another candidate? Maybe some emerging responsibilities need to be added. Revise your description until it describes what you truly want in the next hire.

- **Experience and skills.** What degrees, certificates, or work experience does this person need? Think creatively. Historically, companies tried to find people with similar experience in similar industries. Many leaders now realize the benefits of hiring people with "non-traditional" experience, and list possible alternative qualifications. Perhaps someone from a related but different industry would have a fresh perspective and valuable insights.

- **Personal characteristics.** Be sure to list the attributes that reflect organizational values and are consistent with your organizational values and managerial style: If you need a self-starter, team player, or independent thinker, be sure that's included.[48]

Remember that, when it comes to writing job descriptions, there are no right or wrong answers. Any leader who carefully reviews and updates descriptions stands a better chance of making the right hire.

*Interview effectively*

Once you've solicited applications from many well-qualified candidates through your own recruitment and networking, you're ready to talk to candidates.

This is where many managers go wrong, with no plan or purpose for the interviews.

Standardizing the interview process yields better results. When you ask everyone the same questions, you can easily cross-compare candidates. You might design one question to scan for communication skills, while another assesses their managerial capabilities, and yet another their compatibility with organizational culture. There's another advantage to standardizing your questions and evaluation process: This approach can help counter any subliminal biases that might affect your decision or that of the other interviewers.

Throughout your hiring process, you want to avoid bias for many reasons. First, outright biases can be illegal. Screening out candidates that are parts of certain groups or clients with disabilities or preferences can quickly land you in hot water. Be sure to hire in an ethical and legal way. Second and even more important: Biases often cause hiring managers to overlook diverse candidates, who can bring vital fresh perspectives to the organization. Lastly, being aware of and taking steps to remove bias will improve your overall skills as a leader—an added benefit of the practice.

Start with resumes. When you review resumes, remove names and addresses, to neutralize any possible subconscious reactions you might have. Don't hesitate to ask for work samples, if appropriate. This puts the focus on performance and gives you highly relevant information on which to judge candidates.

---

**EXAMPLE: Seeing candidates for who they are**

One of us served on a team to hire new business consultants. As part of the process, each candidate was given a business case to analyze. Each candidate was interviewed with the same questions and did the same case study. All the interviewers then convened to decide who to bring to headquarters for second-round interviews.

One of the grads, Nate, landed close to the top of the list. His analysis was brilliant, and he was quickly invited for an office visit. Imagine the reaction of the HR team when Nate called to share his travel arrangements and mentioned that he was blind.

As it turned out, Nate was simply the best interviewee among all the candidates. No one had been asked to evaluate based on vision or any other physical ability—the team was simply required to evaluate candidate performance with the case study.

The focus on anonymized analysis of candidates' work led to the best choice. Standardization works.

---

Once you've used a consistent, bias-free process to identify and hire the best talent, you have the raw material needed to build a great team. Next you must find ways to help your team grow their skills and create pathways for advancement.

## Develop

Whether a team member just arrived at your organization or has been there for years, they'll almost certainly want to expand their knowledge and move up in the organization. Your job is to identify their strengths and provide professional development opportunities. Employees rarely leave if they're receiving these opportunities as well as job advancement opportunities.

Robust talent development programs build company loyalty. Further, people want leaders who know them as a whole person, as discussed in our relationship-building chapter. If a team member lives to run marathons on weekends, you want to know that. When they ask for one Friday off a month for race prep, you'll know why and be able to help them keep their career moving forward while still making time for their personal passions.

To start, let's look at how to develop new hires.

### Set up new hires for success

To increase your success in engaging and retaining new hires, use a systematic onboarding process, says Michael Watkins, a professor in leadership and organizational change at Switzerland's IMD Business School, and author of "7 Ways to Set Up a New Hire for Success."[49] Watkins' research found that a consistent onboarding routine brings new employees up to speed 50% faster, reduces washouts who quickly leave, and increases employee engagement.

Once they're on board, it's critical to equip new hires for success. One way organizations do this is by assigning every new employee a *guide*—a colleague they can turn to for help during their first few weeks on the job. The guide should be able to answer all kinds of questions, ranging from how to use the company Wi-Fi to where the bathrooms are located. Assigning guides is straightforward, eases onboarding anxiety, and helps build morale across the organization.

Regular check-ins help too. Schedule lunches and check-in meetings so fledgling employees feel supported and can gauge how well they are progressing in their new roles. This also provides a means to building relationships that stick. Employees who feel their boss and the organization are committed to their success have a greater chance of succeeding that those who don't, so be mindful of these small investments, which can pay huge dividends over time.

### *Conduct technical skills training*

With the rapid pace of change today, both new hires and long-time employees need technical training to keep their job-specific skills sharp. Regardless of whether that training is in new accounting pronouncements, next-generation software applications, changes in procurement regulations, or updated immigration laws (to note only a few), it's essential that employees are proficient in the key aspects of their work.

The good news is there are more ways than ever before to acquire or enhance a technical skill, including online courses, in-classroom work, peer sharing, and learning on the job. While leaders will want to balance efficiency and effectiveness, what matters most is which mode delivers the best skill enhancement.

Be mindful that a simple training program may not be sufficient. Knowledge will be best retained if people learn in a structured format, apply the skills in the workplace, and then reflect on successes and opportunities for improvement. They then repeat the process. This is true for both technical and leadership training.

## *Build leadership-skills training*

Professional development is not all about learning technical skills. Any leader looking to climb the ranks must develop leadership skills, and the Twelve Skills outlined in this book are the most essential. While some people still hold on to the notion that leaders are born not made, we know differently. *Everyone* can improve their leadership skills if they try.

Aside from reading this book or other publications, how can leaders build their skills? There are a few ways.

Keep in mind that leadership is a craft. The same as any trade, the way to improve is by doing it. Identify leadership opportunities for your team. Find out what skills they have an interest in developing, and match those to the needs of the business. If someone wants to improve how they lead project teams, having them take a course is great, but giving them a project to lead is even better. That way they'll learn firsthand how a project works (and in some cases doesn't) through application, feedback, reflection, and reengagement. Don't be afraid to let your team work on things outside their comfort zone, especially if it's something they're interesting in. This will not only enhance their leadership skills but will improve their job satisfaction as well. Share leadership broadly, and over time you will accumulate a team of broadly skilled leaders.

### *Don't neglect development*

We understand that people are busier than ever before. To-do lists aren't getting any shorter, and the hours in a day sure haven't increased. It's easy to let development fall by the wayside as day-to-day demands mount, but resist the temptation.

If you haven't had a focus on professional development for your team, it's time to start. The benefits include:

- **Ensuring team members can handle their jobs**, leading to more efficient processes and increased customer satisfaction

- **Creating a culture of continuous learning** so staff keep up with industry advancements
- **Building a stable of promotion-ready staff** as you grow
- **Making employees feel valued**, thereby improving retention

Active employee development enriches everyone's work life. As noted in the final point on the list above, investments in skill building makes employees feel important and that they have a future with the company, and incentivizes them to stick around. In short: Professional development and advancement build loyalty—something every employer is looking to improve today.

## Coach

To develop talent, you need to do two things: Give your team feedback and help them improve. Sounds easy, right? It should be, especially as there are many books on how to give performance feedback. However, the biggest challenge with feedback isn't usually mentioned in a book. It's the fact that most managers don't like to give feedback, and worse—many don't do it at all.

As you probably know already, it's hard to help people improve if they don't get candid feedback about their performance. Without it, your employees operate in the dark with no idea whether their work is outstanding or terrible. Fortunately, there are ways to make performance feedback constructive and actionable, and that's where we'll start.

## About feedback

Like many topics, there's conflicting research regarding feedback. Some articles discuss how constructive feedback dampens employee performance, while others say it helps. Different research finds that feedback isn't as effective as coaching. Finally, evidence suggests that managers think they're good at coaching, when in fact, most lack the necessary skills. Giving effective feedback can feel challenging enough without all these contradictory thoughts.

Where to begin? We'll blend our most useful findings from research with our experience as coaches, to help clarify the topic and get you on the path to developing your team effectively.

Let's start with three facts:

1. **Employees want feedback.** While we may think employees would rather be left alone, there is compelling evidence that people *want* feedback—both positive and negative.
2. **You need to overcome fears.** The biggest challenge with feedback is helping managers overcome barriers to providing it.

3. **Delivery style makes a major difference.** The way feedback is given has a huge impact on how it is received.

In their article "Your Employees Want the Negative Feedback You Hate to Give," consultants Jack Zenger and Joseph Folkman asked almost 900 leaders their preferences for giving and receiving feedback. The findings are shown in the following figure.

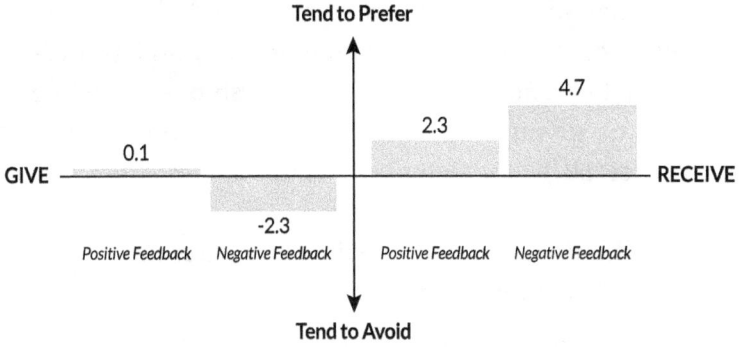

*Preferences for giving and receiving feedback*[50]

Zenger and Folkman found that most people have a slight preference for giving positive feedback, paired with a desire to avoid negative feedback—not a surprising result. However, when it comes to receiving feedback, those same respondents stated that they wanted feedback, regardless of whether it was positive or negative, and that they preferred corrective-type feedback. Why? Because it helps them improve.

How the feedback is given makes a difference, though. The authors explain that people see constructive criticism as essential to their career development, but that leaders often don't feel comfortable giving it. Giving corrective feedback constructively is therefore one of the critical keys to leadership that could set you apart from other leaders.

### *The how of feedback*

How can managers deliver feedback effectively, in a way that addresses corrective needs and also—when called for—provides congratulatory support? According to the Center for Creative Leadership, an effective tool for giving feedback is the Situation-Behavior-Impact (SBI)™ framework, as follows:

- **Situation.** Provides the time and place in which the behavior occurred
- **Behavior.** Describes the behavior—what was seen and heard
- **Impact.** Highlights the effects of the behavior in terms of thoughts, feelings, or actions[51]

This framework helps leaders provide clear, understandable feedback—either positive or corrective—in a direct and professional manner. While every moment of a feedback conversation may not fit tidily into the SBI structure, it is an effective way to frame the conversation and engage in a two-way dialogue in a productive and non-judgmental way. Try it for yourself.

## *The case for coaching*

Some may wonder why coaching is even necessary. If leaders are skilled at giving feedback, why not just focus on that? Our response: The past is not the future. Giving someone feedback about how they performed in the past is not the same as helping them identify how to be successful in the future. That is the role of coaching.

As popular as coaching is, many managers are not good at it, even though most think they are. How can that be, when so many managers have forged successful careers? It boils down to a simple distinction between coaching and supervising.

A supervisor sets expectations, ensures accountability, and drives professional development. Employees do what they can and bring the hard stuff to their supervisors, who tell them what to do (or do it for them). In the minds of many managers, problem solving is synonymous with coaching, but that's not the case—the two are virtually opposites of each other. Problem solving builds dependent employees, and coaching builds independent problem solvers. Guess which one you want on your team.

Supervisors in problem-solving mode usually give advice or direction. The faster the supervisor can give the right answer, the happier everyone is. Supervisors feel smart; employees feel helped.

By contrast, coaches don't give answers, because they presuppose employees can find their own solutions. As a coach, a manager doesn't solve employee problems—even if they are organizational issues—at all. Instead, a good leader asks questions to help employees think through how to resolve challenges on their own. Coaching helps people find their own way to achieve their full potential.

To truly develop talent, you need to stop supervising and start coaching. It may feel frustrating at first, but it's a true win–win for everyone. Employees develop new skills and autonomy. Managers get more capable and engaged teams.

### *A model for coaching*

As executive coaches, we recognize most people won't have the time or interest in going through the training to become a professional coach. The good news is you don't have to. Like feedback, there is a simple framework that works well. After you provide feedback, coach your team using the four-step GROW model.

In Richard Dool's book, *Leaderocity: Leading at the Speed of Now*, Lloyd Pearson and Ngwa Numfor discuss how to use what they call the "simple but purposeful" GROW model. It's a good way to help an employee think through the steps they need to execute to improve.

## STRENGTHENING TALENT DEVELOPMENT

### GROW Model[52]

| | |
|---|---|
| **Goals** | What does the employee what to achieve? First, you and your employee need to look at the behavior that you want to change. and then structure this change as a goal that the mentee wants to achieve. Make sure that this is a SMART goal: One that is Specific, Measurable, Attainable, Realistic, and Time bound. |
| Current **Reality** | What are the current circumstances the employee faces, in relation to the goals they have set? This is an important step. Too often, mentees try to solve a problem or reach a goal without fully considering the starting point, and often they're missing some information that they need to reach their goal effectively. They may be treating a symptom and not the root issue. |
| **Options** (or obstacles) | This is where the manager uses their skills, experience, and expertise to assist the employee in framing their options and how best to navigate them. It is imperative at this stage that the goals be completely the employee's own. |
| **Will** (or way forward) | Finally, setting realistic milestones. What is to be done, with whom, and how? It is the mentor's responsibility to hold the mentee accountable over the course of the mentoring period. By examining the current reality and exploring the options, your mentee will now have a good idea of how they can achieve their goal. But in itself, this may not be enough. The final step is to get the mentee to commit to specific actions to move toward the goal. |

This model is not only straightforward, it also puts the power to improve squarely in the hands of the person being coached rather than in those of the manager. Also, serving as a coach for your team members takes your relationships to a new level—one where you're highly valued for enabling your people to progress in their careers. Once you've given feedback and coached your people, they will go forth and do. Your next job is to help them do better in a more formal, systematized way.

## Manage

Looking holistically at talent development, you have one simple goal: To help your people grow professionally. The result of helping people develop is two-fold. First, you have satisfied employees, who feel valued and enriched. Second, you have a high-performing organization. Unfortunately, many leaders feel the same level of engagement in the performance management process overall as they do in providing individual feedback or coaching—they're not interested.

Fortunately, recent thinking on performance management points to more effective ways to help your direct reports. From the age-old focus of holding employees accountable for their results, performance management has evolved into a framework for learning, say Wharton management professor Peter Cappelli and New York University human-capital professor Anna Tavis in their article "The Performance Management Revolution."[53]

## What is performance management?

Performance management is the process where managers talk with employees and align employees' goals to those of the business. The manager then monitors and rewards progress through the entire year, or through the cycle for that goal.

In some organizations, the annual review has been replaced by a continuous process of quick, informal progress check-ins, coupled with frequent rewards for hitting milestones. The approaches we've highlighted in this chapter align with this thinking. It allows for more rapid course correction and makes the improvement process an ongoing dialogue versus a periodic event.

The employee receives many reminders about their goals and knows managers review progress often. It's a vast improvement over spending months dreading a single, scripted annual review that spotlights your failings, when it's often too late to fix problems.

## The performance management cycle

To boil it down, this approach to performance management has four basic steps, as you see in the following figure.

*Performance management cycle*

1. **Plan:** Start by helping employees develop a plan for improvement. This plan has specific goals, aligned to competencies (if the organization has them), discrete actions, and a timeline for their completion.

2. **Monitor:** The employee and the manager monitor performance, focusing mainly on completing actions according to plan.

3. **Review:** Because performance management works best as a continuous process rather than via a single annual meeting, ongoing reviews are held at logical increments (for example, monthly) to gauge progress. As goals are accomplished, new goals can be added and obstacles can be addressed.

4. **Reward:** As employees complete their actions and achieve their goals, rewards can be given, aligned with the organization's compensation approach.

With dynamic performance management, employees are more aware of expectations. Skills can be enhanced and resources provided as needed. Leaders should not only manage this process for their subordinates but also enthusiastically participate in a performance management cycle with their own boss and colleagues. Modeling this behavior is the true sign of a leader, as it shows your belief in the value of continuous learning and improvement.

## Getting started with talent development

Here you reviewed our four-step HDCM process for becoming a talent developer: Hire, Develop, Coach, and Manage. You also learned the targeted way to improve various aspects of people development, from interviewing tips to providing better feedback.

Follow these ideas to further jumpstart the process:

- **Become magnetic.** A talent magnet is someone who attracts capable employees to them. Many employees' top complaint is that the company does not invest in their development. Regardless of what your organization does, you can always make the commitment to be a talent magnet.

- **Make the time.** Like growing a garden, developing your people takes time and commitment. Calendar your time and make development a priority.

- **Ask for input.** You don't have to do all the heavy lifting yourself. Ask your team to provide their own thoughts on how you can help them in their own development.

The bottom line is that great leaders understand the importance of managing talent. It's not something they do in addition to their job—it's a key part of their job. As you offer team members the chance to learn and grow, they see more purpose and meaning in their work, feel they're making a difference, and become more committed to the organization. Staff turnover is reduced and you build stronger relationships with your direct reports.

Once you're committed to developing your people, you're ready to help them come together as a team to achieve goals, working as a highly effective, cohesive unit. That's the skill we'll talk about next.

# 7
# Invigorating Team Building

Have you noticed that you rarely do tasks all by yourself these days? It's not your imagination—there are more teams in the work world now than ever before, and that trend will only grow in the future.

Today's organizations are highly collaborative, both inside the company and with outside partners, which we'll discuss in the next chapter. Given how firms have grown in terms of their global scale and scope, driven by advances in meeting technology, teaming has become the standard for getting work done. That means leading teams is no longer a skill left to the experts—everyone must be good at it. Unfortunately, little time is spent learning how to lead a team effectively—it's a more complex task than managing people one to one. To succeed, you need to assemble the right people, set direction, and manage the team development process. You'll of course also need to deliver the results the team was chartered to achieve.

## Why team building?

Still not bought in as to why team-building skills are so important? Deloitte's 2019 Human Capital Trends shows that 35% of executives reported they already work almost wholly in teams, while another 65% said they do some of their work in cross-functional teams.[54] As the era of top-down management declines, hierarchies are being replaced by teams across industries and geographies. Companies are becoming increasingly networked as employment structures fill with freelancers, vendors, and other partners. Managing this kind of diversity is no mean feat, so it's important that leaders have strong team-building skills.

Another often overlooked aspect of team building is talent development. Because people are spending their time at work on teams, much of the feedback they receive will come from their various team leaders, not their immediate supervisors. In some cases, an administrative supervisor may not even work directly with an employee. Team leaders are therefore increasingly the ones to provide feedback and give coaching.

Talent development and team building go hand in hand today. To succeed as a leader, you need to get the best from everybody and keep people focused on a shared goal. This isn't as easy as it looks—team dysfunction is an epidemic. If you apply *any* of the skills we outline in this chapter, you will be well ahead of the competition.

## Chapter goals

In this chapter we'll outline the basics of teams: What they are, how they work, and where they go wrong. We'll also give you a process for launching and developing a team.

Using the tools we provide, you will be able to:

- Describe and design the successful configuration of a team
- Launch and develop a team, using a structured process
- Perform the basic responsibilities of a team leader
- Spot the common dysfunctions of a team and plan to mitigate them

---

**EXERCISE: Team Building—self-assessment**

There's a good chance you're leading a team right now. If that's the case, how are you faring as a team leader? Take a minute to complete this short assessment to give yourself an idea of your current capabilities.

Rate yourself using the following scale:
0: Never, 1: Occasionally, 2: Often, 3: Always

| Team building—self-assessment | | | | |
|---|---|---|---|---|
| I ensure the team has the right people on it to enable success. | 0 | 1 | 2 | 3 |
| I set clear guidance so that we deliver on our team purpose and goals. | 0 | 1 | 2 | 3 |
| I create a safe environment where performance is encouraged, strong relationships flourish, team processes are effective, and conflict is managed. | 0 | 1 | 2 | 3 |
| Total score | | | | |

If you scored 7 or more, you're likely leading your team effectively. Well done. If you scored yourself 5 or 6, you have implemented some worthwhile team practices but can add a few more. If you rated yourself 4 or below you have a significant opportunity to enhance your team's performance.

If your team leadership is falling short of where you'd like it, don't fret. This chapter will help you quickly generate measurable improvements.

## Team defined

Most of us are so deeply involved in the work of our teams that we rarely think about what a team is (or what it should be). Harvard Business School's Working Knowledge article "The Importance of

Teaming" defines a team as follows: "A team is an established, fixed group of people cooperating in pursuit of a common goal."[55]

That's a straightforward description. The problem is most teams aren't teams at all. They're working groups: People working together without the cooperation, commitment, and unity of a real team. Not that there's anything wrong with a group of people working together—sometimes that's required by the task. Think of a committee chartered to explore the impact of a new government regulation—their mandate might purely be to report findings. A high-performing team isn't required in a situation like this.

## Elements of a real team

While our definition of a team provides a useful baseline, it's not sufficient to determine whether you have built a real team. In their article "The Discipline of Teams," Jon Katzenbach and Doug Smith list five characteristics that comprise a bona fide team:

- **A mix of complementary skills.** Team members should have a mix of technical and/or functional expertise, problem-solving and decision-making skills, and interpersonal skills. Skills mix should be added to or changed as the work requirements shift.

- **A meaningful common purpose.** While teams are put together for many reasons, successful teams have a meaningful purpose that each member connects with.

- **Specific performance goals.** The common purpose drives a set of performance goals that inspires the team and gives them a sense of urgency regardless of titles or seniority.

- **A strong commitment to how the work gets done.** Teams need to be clear on roles, responsibilities, and routines and must adhere to them. Everyone needs to be included and feel a sense of obligation to the team's success.

- **Mutual accountability.** Trust and commitment are essential elements of every successful team. The process of working through trials and tribulations engenders a sense of accountability to one another.[56]

These five characteristics are time-tested and easy to understand—they have proven to be essential elements of high-performing teams. We'll refer to them as we work through this chapter.

## Skill builder Seven: 3D team-building process

Getting to the point where your team is high-performing isn't rocket science. There are a few practices that will make most, if not all, of the difference. To help accelerate the process, we've developed a simple three-step rubric to building an effective team, which incorporates what we've discussed at the outset.

Below is our 3D framework for developing your own high-performing team:

1. **Design:** Recruit the right mix of skills and personalities to enable team success.

2. **Direction:** Steer and coach team members to achieve team goals.

3. **Dynamics:** Build relationships, create a safe space, and defuse conflicts.

A thoughtfully assembled team with positive dynamics, where all team members have a shared sense of purpose and understand the goal, stands the best chance of success. If any of these elements are missing, the team flounders.

Let's look at best practices in each step of the process so you can enhance your team-management skills where needed.

## Design

Success begins with selecting the right team members. The upfront design is vital. We'll discuss how to select team members; the most effective size of teams; team charters, roles and responsibilities; and accelerating team development. A team with the right mix (and number) of people, who are clear on what they're doing and why, is on track to do great work together.

### *Selecting team members*

As noted by Katzenbach and Smith, team members should have a mix of technical and functional expertise, problem-solving and decision-making skills, and interpersonal skills.

Think of how Marvel's Avengers use their different superpowers together to save the world. While your mandate may not be as daunting, you still need the right mix of capabilities to support your purpose and achieve your goals. Ask yourself, *What skills are required to achieve our team's mission?* Your team then needs to assemble that blend of skills in a way that provides the best chance for a positive outcome.

For instance, imagine you recruit a team made up entirely of skilled scientists. While they all likely have different areas of technical expertise, they may have common inclinations and similar training. A team of people who all have the same inclinations may not communicate well if the team were to hit roadblocks. It's possible no one would check in with peers to coordinate actions.

Diversity of thought, experience, and perspective is vitally important on teams. Personalities, styles, and strengths need to be recognized, so the team can get the best from everyone. Each team member should have clarity on their part in achieving the goal. Consider writing a role description for each member's responsibilities within the team.

## *Team size*

Have you ever wondered about the right size for a team? Some studies put the ideal range for productive teams at between three and ten people. Beyond that, group cohesion usually breaks down—there are too many people to coordinate with for the team to operate optimally. Jeff Bezos has a famous team-size heuristic, called the *two-pizza rule*, where the optimal team size is one that can be fed by two pizzas. Food for thought for any team leader.

## *Creating a team charter*

Once you have people with complementary skills on board, you want to get them focused and engaged, using a team charter. According to Harvard Business School's guide *Creating Teams with an Edge*, a team charter is a concise, written document that specifies some or all of the following:

- Name of project sponsor
- Relationship and priority of the team's work to unit or corporate goals
- Expected time frame of the work
- Concise description of project deliverables
- The project's benefits
- The budget, allocations, and resources available to the team
- The team's authority
- The sponsor's signature[57]

Documenting and agreeing on these aspects of a team's design can clarify expectations and help measure progress. It starts people on the path to shared commitment—a fundamental aspect of successful teams. The charter states *what* a team needs to do, but not *how*. Those details are best left to a project plan.

### *Roles and responsibilities*

Operating in today's fast-changing business environment, successful teams tend to have fluid roles that are regularly re-evaluated, notes Harvard organizational-behavior professor Ethan Bernstein in his article, "Leadership and Teaming."[58] The scope of each role must balance needed skills, types of work, and the importance of various tasks. Each member should find their team assignments both meaningful and rewarding.

One often overlooked area of assignments is representation. Whom does each team member represent on this team—the entire company, their business unit, or just themselves individually? Clarity on representation will help each team member feel empowered.

### Accelerating team development

Teams have a life cycle, defined by Bruce Tuckman back in 1965 as "forming, storming, norming, and performing."[59] At the start of team development, your team sits at the formative stage—the time when you select members, develop a charter and specify roles and responsibilities. In the end, the team adjourns when the task is complete. Your job as leader is to accelerate the team's growth toward effective performance so that the team rapidly becomes highly productive. To do that, you need to give clear guidance and direction as well as manage the complex interpersonal issues that arise between your team members.

## Direction

With the right people in place, the team needs clear, consistent guidance on direction. This starts with their purpose and goals. Purpose and goals are the team's north star, pointing them to where they are going and reorienting them if they get lost in the details. As the leader, you need to focus the team on that north star and on building commitment to the work. You also need to keep track of progress and team effectiveness.

### *Purpose and goals*

If teams have an origin story, in the beginning is the purpose. You need to gain agreement and support for why the team should exist and what it needs to do. The team's purpose needs to fit the task, the team, and everyone involved. Your role is to help define the purpose based on the organization's needs and the interests of the members.

Establish the purpose together initially, and the team will revisit and update the purpose throughout the team's lifetime together. For the purpose to be effective, it needs to be meaningful—something the team members will connect with and support each other over, both individually and collectively.

### *Setting clear guidance*

From the purpose flows clear, quantifiable team goals. These state exactly what the team needs to do to succeed. Crisp goals will keep everyone focused, motivated, and mutually accountable for accomplishing them. Effective team leaders avoid confusion by making goals concrete, specific, and—dare we say it—measurable.

As Katzenbach and Smith note, team goals should be compelling and urgent, requiring team members to set aside their differences and to focus on objectives.[60] An example might be halving the product development cycle and getting the next product to market a certain number of weeks faster.

From there, team members must agree on working methods and how they'll hold each other accountable for their tasks. On high-performing teams, work is divided equally, and everyone—including the leader—contributes in concrete ways.

You should continue to guide the team throughout the process, not just at the beginning. Keep bringing new information and facts to the group to refine their knowledge and direction. Early wins allow you to reinforce the team's direction with positive feedback, rewards, and recognition. This quickly takes the team's goals beyond the abstract. The team's work is underway, early movers get rewarded, and everyone should get busy on their own tasks.

## *Building commitment*

Why do team members do their work? They do it because it's their job, yes; but they do it happily if they feel a sense of commitment to the team, its members, and its aims.

Remember to celebrate the team and its accomplishments—not just at the end, when the product development cycle time has been shortened, but also throughout the process. Celebrate when the first milestone is achieved and, yes, celebrate when the team has learned something the hard way. Failure is disappointing but failing and learning quickly creates a victory.

As a leader, be sure to give credit to the whole team for every success. One member may have been out for the birth of his first baby when the deadline was met, but be sure to list him on the team in the company newsletter. Be sure a member's supervisor receives feedback from you for her performance review too. Let everyone know they matter to you and to the team effort.

It's critical to build a positive team culture, where team members bond with each other and feel they're part of something bigger than themselves. When teammates feel that sense of belonging, they'll make sacrifices for the team goals, and sacrifice is often needed in teamwork.

---

**EXAMPLE: Team before self**

One of us swam competitively in college. At a particularly important meet with a rival, our coach pulled one of our swimmers aside and asked them to take it easy on their first, individual race (risking a loss) so they would be fresh for a later, longer race. Without this swimmer's help, the team would be weaker in that later race, and they needed a victory there to win the meet. The swimmer focused on the second race, committing to the team's results rather than to their own top performance.

Your goal as leader should be to build this sort of team—a team that everyone loves being on and is willing to make sacrifices for. On a work team, that might mean putting in late nights coding, or sticking with a difficult research assignment. The work of each team member is important because it drives the shared team success. The work *matters*.

---

When the team project ends, you want to hear that members wish this team could keep going because they loved being part of your team. Commitment makes people feel valuable, and they don't want it to end.

## *Measuring team effectiveness*

Effective teams must do one thing: Accomplish their goals. To know if that's happening, you need to measure progress as your team project goes along. We describe the best performance-measurement techniques in Chapter 11, but we want to note a few team-specific issues here.

The end goal isn't the only thing a team leader needs to measure. There should be many milestones along the way that offer chances to assess whether the project is

**TWELVE SKILLS**

on track. There are also process and personal-development goals to monitor. Are the processes the team agreed on working well, or do they need improvement? Is the team functioning well, with strong interpersonal relationships between team members? Finally, are team members being developed? These are all areas to monitor and measure.

Members should feel they're becoming better professionals because of being on the team. At the end of a high-performing team's work, members have the sense of accomplishment and of completing difficult tasks together, and—ideally—have grown relationships and their own careers along the way.

## Dynamics

Once the team has recruited diverse members, created its purpose, set goals, and started its work, it's time to optimize the team's processes. The good leader fosters positive interpersonal relationships among the team members and ensures the team uses time efficiently and effectively in meetings. Conflict and interpersonal challenges must be managed, and the leader needs to pay attention to team members' interactions. Finally, but as important as anything else, team members need to build their own skills. The team's success depends on team dynamics and the leader's skill. That's where we'll turn first.

## *Team leader responsibilities*

The team leader plays the most critical role in a team's success, but what does the leader do? Good team leaders play many roles, but six activities demand most of their attention:

1. **Creating trust and safety:** Fostering an environment where team members feel they can share information freely and participate to the best of their abilities

2. **Building dyadic relationships:** Getting to know each person on the team in a meaningful way

3. **Understanding and managing conflict:** Working to enable the sharing and resolving of differences in a productive way

4. **Holding efficient, effective meetings:** Ensuring the primary work forum is high-functioning

5. **Providing feedback, coaching, and development:** Taking the time to let people know how they're doing and improve their skills

6. **Learning from before- and after-action reviews:** Checking periodically to gauge what's working and what needs improvement

Great leaders don't put together a team and then wander off to other projects. They guide the team throughout its life span by focusing on the main drivers of goal achievement.

## Creating trust and safety

For your team to be effective, you need to build trust among teammates, creating a safe space in which to voice opinions. That might sound like a tall order, but there are in fact two things that make a huge difference. A few years ago, Google researched team effectiveness. Dubbed Project Aristotle, the research found two things were vital to creating a feeling of psychological safety: Giving each member equal time to voice opinions, and high average social sensitivity. Not talking over colleagues and taking turns also means team members learn more and understand their team members better—another trust builder. Also social sensitivity: an ability to read how others are feeling based on non-verbal skills such as facial expression or body language. If you have a truly diverse team, this will be even more important, as team members need to understand each other's perspectives, vocabulary, and embedded assumptions.[61]

## Building dyadic relationships

A lot of the success in team leadership flows from understanding each team member and what makes them tick. To manage team dynamics, the leader needs to build a one-on-one relationship with each member. A team is a group of people, but team members must develop relationships individually. You can't calm down an angry person or cheer up a discouraged person, if you don't know what's important to them and what motivates them. Invest the time to get to know each of your team members personally. It will be well worth the effort.

## Understanding and managing conflict

When two people work together, sooner or later, a disagreement will arise. Now imagine the impact when a team of diverse people are together—the effect is multiplied. For a team to succeed, conflict has to be resolved quickly. Good teams have three important features, a University of Virginia report found: The team achieves its goals; the collaboration process sets the team up for future wins; and members feel they personally benefit from being on the team.[62] Sadly, the report also found that, five weeks into their projects, only 25% of teams achieved all three outcomes. What got in the way? Unresolved conflicts. Good team leaders forecast possible conflict scenarios and proactively plan ways to resolve problems. That way, leaders are prepared and can move quickly to neutralize a disagreement before it becomes an obstacle to team effectiveness.

## Holding efficient, effective meetings

Ask anyone on a team how it's going, and they will no doubt share an anecdote from one of their team meetings. Meetings are the main forum where most teams interact. That might lead you to believe it's the most effective too. Not true. Many teams meet too often, for the wrong purposes, and with poor organization, so their meetings have no tangible benefit. That's unfortunate, since practices for running team meetings effectively haven't changed for decades.

In his time-tested *Harvard Business Review* article, "How to Run a Meeting," Antony Jay provides a miniature manifesto on how to plan and execute effective meetings. Things to consider in advance:

- **Purpose.** Is the meeting to share information, to make decisions, or to work together?

- **Frequency.** How often should we meet—daily, weekly, monthly, if recurring? If not recurring, what should trigger a meeting?

- **Preparation.** How will we prepare for the meeting—setting objectives, responsibilities, deciding attendance, for example?

- **Roles.** What are participants' roles? (For example, chairperson or participant)

- **Discussion.** What is the structure of the discussion (order and flow of topics) and how will participants engage?

- **Conduct.** How do we ensure everyone is engaged and no one dominates?

- **Closing.** How will we close the meeting and follow up afterward, for example, sending of minutes and tracking action items?[63]

As you can see, quite a lot goes into effective meetings. If you don't have good processes in place, the team tends to break down. It's therefore important to define the meetings you have, with clear expectations of what you will accomplish. At the same time, it's important that team members do not spend too much time meeting—especially when your team is large, every member may not need to attend every time.

If the team is having a challenge with meetings, bring together the affected members to learn new approaches together.

### Providing feedback, coaching, and development

A key factor that separates high-performing teams from inefficient working groups is members feeling satisfied in being part of the team. The team leader needs to build that feeling by providing professional development opportunities as the team's work progresses. One way members grow is through feedback. It should be a two-way street, with feedback flowing not just from you to team members, but also from them back to you. Model that you are also learning and growing as the team works toward its goal. Coaching is also part of development, as we discuss in the coaching section of Chapter 6. As you build your dyadic relationships, you may also begin to coach team members.

People learn through mistakes, so leaders need to make the team a safe space for striving, failing, learning, and moving forward. Team members are unlikely to experiment if there's ongoing conflict, which is a key reason conflict must be resolved quickly, say organizational-behavior professors Kristin Behfar and Rebecca Goldberg in their case study "Conflict Management in Teams."[64]

If multiple team members are struggling, it may be time to stop and learn new ways to work together. Organize a learning meeting, or a session where members give each other constructive feedback, to build that feeling of team commitment. Then work resumes.

Ideally, the meeting will be in person. If that's not possible, meet via videoconference if you need to talk strategy, learn a new skill, or do a task that needs real-time discussion. People need to be able to see each other and read others' body language to keep relationships growing.

### *Learning from before- and after-action reviews*

Spawned from the military's need to learn and improve during battle, after-action reviews (AARs) have become a business staple. Many leaders have learned to analyze a project's success or failure on completion, but far fewer executives derive meaningful lessons from the process to help them avoid future problems.

How can you make sure your team learns from what you've accomplished (or what you've struggled with)? First, consider a *before-action review* at the start, taking time to pull up past AARs and extract lessons from them. Once you're underway, mini-AARs should take place at each project milestone. Once you've identified areas for improvement, discuss how you will avoid repeating errors. Decide how team members will be held accountable for implementing what you've learned.

## Managing virtual teams

Between pandemic isolation and business globalization, the need for virtual teams has grown exponentially. Sometimes it may not even be possible to meet in person due to geographic, health, and other issues. How can you make your virtual team effective?

Leaders of virtual teams can bridge the gap if they foster trust, encourage open dialogue, and set clear guidelines. It's also important to keep virtual meetings focused and to the point. As beneficial as online meeting platforms have become, keep in mind that everyone can only take so much time on Zoom, Teams, Webex, or Google Meet (or other videoconferencing platforms). When planning and executing virtual events, keep in mind that virtual interaction doesn't hold our attention the way in-person conversations do.

To keep team members engaged in the virtual world, encourage multiple forms of interaction. For instance, shy teammates can use the chat function to contribute ideas. The leader can react to chat during or after the meeting. The leader can also save and distribute the chat log to all participants, making sure ideas are given equal weight.

Virtual teams often accomplish much of their work asynchronously—perhaps posting in Slack, Microsoft Teams, Trello, or other teaming tools as they complete tasks or have questions. It's still important, though, to bring the team together face to face to build connections.

### *When you inherit a team*

So far, we've described the journey new leaders take to build a team from scratch and then manage its performance. However, you may only rarely have that luxury, if ever. Most likely you'll be transferred or promoted and end up managing an existing team that is likely not to be in perfect condition. If this is something you're facing, know that you can reshape an existing team and improve its performance.

First, you need to assess the members based on your criteria—the same ones you would have used if you were starting from scratch. Are they in the right roles, and do they have the right skills? Next, reshape the team lineup, subbing in new players as needed. Establish a clear sense of purpose and direction to reinvigorate the reconstituted team, in alignment with current challenges. Finally, look for some easy, early wins the team can achieve, to build confidence and accelerate team development.

Whether you're managing a team you built yourself or reshaping one you inherited, you need to coach team members to success.

## Avoid common team dysfunctions

What makes teams fail? There are several common reasons teams flounder, as Harvard organizational-behavior professor Ethan Bernstein notes in his article "Leadership and Teaming."[65] For instance, if there's a mismatch between team skills and the team's goal, the team may be unable to deliver the requested results.

Information overload is another common problem that stymies groups. Members spend so much time learning, they can't meet project deadlines. As the leader, you may need to cut off new input or research time at some point to keep the project on track.

Problems in team dynamics can also destroy group cohesion and derail a project. If team members' emotional needs aren't being met, they tend to feel less committed and less motivated to do team tasks.

If there aren't clear ground rules for equal time and turn taking, dominant members may impose their beliefs on others, leading to groupthink rather than a diversity of ideas. If the environment doesn't feel safe, members will self-censor and not actively participate.

You can see why we've spotlighted the importance of managing team dynamics—there are many ways poor team interactions can cause your team to fail at its mission.

## Getting started with team building

In this chapter you explored our 3D approach for becoming a great team leader—Design, Direction, and Dynamics. You delved into each one, adding what you should be doing as a leader and what you want to avoid to your toolkit on team leadership.

You're now to the point where you can confidently up your team leader game. Below are a few things to keep in mind as you do:

- **Gauge effectiveness.** It's easy to get stuck in the day-to-day monotony of teamwork without assessing team effectiveness. Review your charter and goals (first creating these if you don't have them) to check you're on track.

- **Check in with team members.** Team members' personal situations change daily. Check in with people frequently to make sure they are physically, mentally, and emotionally intact.

- **Hone the team process.** Teamwork can be tiring, especially when it's not efficient. Attend to the team process and dynamics to ensure your routines are optimal.

As you've discovered, effective leaders build high-performing teams by engaging in thoughtful team design, providing the team with clear direction, and carefully managing the team's process and personal dynamics. Master the three Ds, and you'll keep driving your team toward higher levels of performance.

Now you have the tools to assemble high-performing teams, you're ready to tackle another skill great leaders need: The ability to collaborate between teams, both internally and outside of your organization.

# 8
# Improving Group Collaboration

It used to be that many organizations waited for senior leaders to provide the guidance needed to complete tasks before employees rallied to fulfill the CEO's directives. That's not how organizations operate today. People and resources are no longer centrally controlled—globalization requires distributed leadership. To provide customer-focused solutions, organizations need collaboration across functions, across multiple organizations, and even across multiple industries, to coordinate activities and generate innovative ideas for future success.

The big-box retailer Best Buy provides a good example. When it was founded, Best Buy was simply a store selling tech products. More than a decade after opening their doors, they introduced the Geek Squad, offering installation and repair services for the products they sold. Today, Best Buy's service division offers a broad array of help, including data recovery, spyware removal, media-room design, and product recycling. To grow in this way, Best Buy collaborated both inside and outside of the company with people who know the tech-services sector, to acquire service expertise and create this new division.

## Why collaboration?

Thanks to new technology, the pandemic, and the rise in demand for skilled workers around the globe, collaboration—together with knowing how to collaborate—has become increasingly important. According to Rob Cross, Babson College professor and an expert in collaboration, the need for coloration has never been greater. "Practically everything we do at work is a collaboration. Pre-pandemic, many people spent 85% or more of their time each week in collaborative work—answering emails, instant messaging, in meetings, and using other team collaboration tools and spaces."[66]

This number has only grown throughout the pandemic, with no end in sight as we move into various forms of hybrid work. Jennifer Moss, a work expert, noted in her article, "The Pandemic Changed Us. Now Companies Have to Change Too," that a 2022 Microsoft study of work trends recognized that between February 2020 and February 2022:

- Weekly team meetings increased by 252%
- Six billion more emails were sent
- People were chatting 32% more frequently
- The average after-hours work increased by 28%[67]

This poses an unusually complex management challenge: Handling the increased volume of collaboration while paying close attention to workforce burnout. This offers rising leaders excellent opportunities for reputation building, both inside your organization and beyond. Even joining a collaboration as a participant can provide opportunities to step up and lead some aspect of the group's work. Collaborations also help diversify your network. In short: Collaborative efforts in organizations are essential to both current and future success, and leaders need to have strong collaboration skills to be successful.

Becoming skilled at participating in and leading a major collaboration requires muscle—the kind that can be strengthened with practice. That's why we've included it in our set of Twelve Skills.

## Chapter goals

The world marketplace has changed, requiring ever-increasing levels of collaboration. The collaborations you work on will also continue to grow in complexity.

The tools we introduce in this chapter will help you:

- Recognize when you need to collaborate (and when you don't)
- Assemble a group of people that will collaborate effectively
- Guide your project successfully and manage conflict
- Make collective progress toward defined goals

---

**EXERCISE: Collaboration—self-assessment**

If your organization is like many we work with, you're probably currently overseeing some type of collaborative effort. If that's the case, you need to ask yourself how effectively you are leading or guiding the effort. Quickly review our short assessment to get a sense of how skillfully you're contributing today.

Rate yourself using the following scale:
0: Never, 1: Occasionally, 2: Often, 3: Always

| Collaboration—self-assessment | | | | |
|---|---|---|---|---|
| My collaboration has a diverse group of creative thinkers who are outcome-oriented. | 0 | 1 | 2 | 3 |
| The process we use is structured and has activities that guide success and reward efforts. | 0 | 1 | 2 | 3 |

| | | | | |
|---|---|---|---|---|
| We foster broad-based participation and monitor and measure progress toward the achievement of defined goals. | 0 | 1 | 2 | 3 |
| Total score | | | | |

If you scored 7 or greater, you're likely guiding your collaboration with aplomb. If you found yourself in the 5-6 range, you've probably instituted some effective practices but could stand to bolster your work. If you scored yourself 4 or less you may want to review how your group is functioning. In instances where you're not where you want to be, you can make improvements using the processes and practices we've provided in this chapter.

## Collaboration definition

What does it mean to lead a successful collaboration? We like this definition from the article, "Are You a Collaborative Leader?" by London Business School professor Herminia Ibarra and UC Berkeley School of Information professor Morten Hansen: "Collaborative leadership is the capacity to engage people and groups outside one's formal control and inspire them to work toward common goals—despite differences in convictions, cultural values, and operating norms."[68]

As this definition suggests, it's more difficult to lead a collaboration across multiple divisions, companies or even industries than it is to lead an in-house team.

**TWELVE SKILLS**

Think of collaboration leadership as team leadership on steroids. That means our advice from Chapter 7 on leading teams applies here too—have a look at that again, as it's the starting point for our thinking in this chapter.

There are some challenges to collaboration that go beyond what we've discussed already, though. As Ibarra and Hansen mention, you don't control your collaboration partners directly; you might have less in common with them than with your close coworkers, and you may not be working together in ways that you (or they) are used to. Collaboration is likely to be more challenging than their typical day jobs for everyone involved.

If collaboration is so hard, what's the point of it? Rest assured, we're not suggesting you include more stakeholders and shoot for more complex outcomes for no reason. You should collaborate because the outcomes you want *require* it. Collaborations need breakthrough creativity, which requires a broad diversity of experience and knowledge—something beyond the skillset of you and your team; maybe even beyond the abilities of your entire company. That kind of thinking should help you gauge the level of effort—and magnitude of outcomes—your own work should strive for.

## What effective collaboration looks like

A productive collaboration brings together the right resources, people, and ideas to solve a challenge, wherever they are. In an extraordinary recent example, those resources spanned the globe and came from private industry and from the governments of the US, Ukraine, and other Eastern European countries. At the start of Russia's 2022 invasion of Ukraine, Microsoft detected a malware attack affecting the systems of Ukrainian government agencies and banks. Rather than keeping this revelation private and perhaps coding a patch to block the attack and keep their own software secure, Microsoft quickly entered into a groundbreaking collaboration with the affected entities (and other potential targets) to defeat the cyberattack.[69] To accomplish this, some Microsoft employees were granted security clearances to access government intelligence and computers while sharing their own technical knowledge. The mutual exchange helped quickly shut down the attack.

We'll likely need more of these sorts of cross-industry collaborations in the future as geopolitics grows more complex. That's why learning to lead a collaboration now gives you a competitive edge.

You may be thinking that this example sounds nothing like your job. Maybe it isn't. However, this type of work will become increasingly common, and we've seen a lot of it in the organizations we've worked with. If you want to work effectively on big, exciting projects with people who don't report to you or to your bosses, or if you want to find solutions to problems that others haven't been able to solve, you should read on.

TWELVE SKILLS

## When to collaborate (and when not to)

Given the challenges of collaborating across organizations, paired with the volume of work you're likely already drowning in, you might be wondering whether you should even be constructing a collaboration anyway. When is collaboration called for? Here are a few thoughts to keep in mind.

First, ask yourself if the work you need to accomplish can be addressed effectively by an individual or by a small group. Can one person make a strong start on the work? Can two or three people get the bulk of the job done? Sometimes only one or two people are needed to effectively address a pressing issue. (For more on this kind of question, refer to Chapter 2 on problem solving.)

Second, think about whether you need a diverse array of contributors. For instance, do you need to hear from both millennials and baby boomers? North Americans and non-English speakers from developing nations? Senior leaders as well as junior staff? If so, you may need a broader team than could be assembled within your division or even within a large corporation.

Think back to our previous example. Microsoft clearly needed more than two or three people to handle a coordinated Russian cyberattack, and a diverse array of contributors was essential to build a broad solution quickly. However, don't add team members, security clearances, and multiple languages to a project without good reason. Resist the urge to assemble a broad-based team when one isn't needed. This will save everyone valuable time and ease your management burden down the road.

## Skill builder Eight: 3P collaboration process

Collaboration might sound complicated, and it can be. The more important the effort and the more wide-reaching its effects, the bigger and more diverse the group working on the project will need to be, and complexity increases with size. That said, don't worry—we have a roadmap for success that will help you frame and guide your work.

The elements you need can be distilled into three Ps:

1. **People:** Build a diverse group of creative thinkers who focus on outcomes and possess the boldness to envision new solutions.

2. **Process:** Create defined structures and activities that will guide the collaboration to success and

defuse conflict. Incentives properly reward collaborators.

3. **Performance:** Monitor and measure progress toward defined goals, ensuring everyone participates in sharing creative ideas.

If you can master these three elements, you can advance your career by leading collaborations. Let's delve into the specifics of each step so you're equipped to effectively organize, manage, and drive to completion effective collaborative efforts.

## People

Obviously, there can't be a collaboration without a group of people. As a collaboration leader, you need to seek people from varied backgrounds who also possess the needed skills. Having the right mix from the outset puts you on the road to success.

Even if you haven't yet led a major collaboration, you probably have some experience managing diverse teams in-house. Perhaps you've visited emerging markets your organization serves, traveled outside your home country, or networked with people in a different age group. Make diversity a priority in all your work, and you'll have resources at the ready for building a collaborative team. To attract people, however, you need to ensure you have the credibility to be viewed as a leader capable of overseeing a collaborative effort.

## Model collaboration first

Before you invite people to your collaboration, you need to be seen as part of an organization capable of effectively leading a project like this. If this is alien to your company culture, it will be difficult to recruit anyone on your staff to join the collaboration, let alone people from outside your organization. Executives at the highest level in your organization need to be engaged in collaborations across boundaries of company, geography, and industry to show this is a desirable operating model.

Individually, you want to establish a track record as a strong collaborator, even when your organization isn't necessarily inclined to collaboration. What does that look like? You need strong skills in building relationships, developing effective teams, and getting results. These three factors will cement in people's minds your ability not only to work with people effectively, but also to make things happen in your organization.

## Identify the right people

Who are you looking for to staff your collaboration? The obvious answer is the people who have the needed skills and knowledge. More than that, though, Ibarra and Hansen found, you need people who respond well to a collaborative leader.

Collaborative leadership is markedly different from command-and-control (top-down) leadership or leading by consensus. Consensus will stall progress because too many people are involved and collective decision making is too slow. Top-down leadership will suffocate the process because the group's structure is too complex to control directly. Also, top-down leaders tend to hoard information, and collaboration requires sharing knowledge beyond the organization and to all participants. Collaborative leaders therefore have to be more directive than consensus leaders, and they have to share authority and knowledge more than top-down leaders.

Finally, a collaborative leader measures performance against shared goals that extend beyond the organization. Again, this differs between leadership styles. Top-down leaders usually focus on their own organization's financial results, while consensus-based leaders may have a wider variety of performance indicators. The collaborative leadership style is the only way to enable such a diverse enterprise to succeed. Consider what types of leadership your potential collaboration participants are accustomed to as you decide whom to invite.

### *Characteristics of great collaborators*

What makes a great collaborator? You're looking for people who excel at spotting emerging opportunities or generating creative solutions. These are open-minded people who will be comfortable working with and soliciting input from diverse colleagues from all walks of life. Keep in mind, it may not be the people with the most technical competence. They'll need to be effective team players, capable of working in fluid environments, skilled at working to build agreement, and people who contribute well to group work. Along with those skills, make sure candidates have the proper mindset to contribute meaningfully to the project.

## *Overcome defenses*

As you assemble your collaborative group, you'll confront one of the biggest challenges of collaboration: People may not be willing to share their ideas. They're out of their comfort zone, talking to people outside their own organizations. You need to build a sense of shared community, where diverse participants feel safe voicing their wildest thoughts. After all, the point of collaboration is to achieve a breakthrough—that's going to take out-of-the-box thinking.

You want people with completely different world views. You won't get innovative ideas in an environment where participants are worried someone will criticize them for making a suggestion. You may not get full participation either. Establish ground rules that show the collaboration actively encourages radical approaches and "thinking out loud."

## *Extend your networks*

Collaborations present a terrific opportunity to expand your personal network in new directions. People tend to develop networks of people similar to themselves in gender, ethnic background, location, and profession—a narrow network. That means you may not get exposed to much new thinking; you will be in a closed set of people who tend to have similar information and draw similar conclusions to yours. This will limit your development over time. People with broad networks pick up different signals and can bring new and different perspectives. Consider asking possible participants about their networks—are they hearing from some unusual sources? That's ideal for collaboration.

If you have a diverse network now, be sure to tap it to find good people for your collaboration. If your network has limited diversity, make a point of getting to know collaborators who are different from yourself. Extending your network during this collaboration will make it more useful in your next one. You'll gain access to new ideas and broaden your own world view. Read Chapter 5 for more on the fundamentals of effective networking.

## *Build trust*

As we've said above, you need to bind your collaborators together so they feel a sense of community in their work. How do you build that trust?

## IMPROVING GROUP COLLABORATION

Boston Scientific co-founder John Abele outlines three actions to take that help build community and convince collaborators who don't *have* to work together to do so:

- Inspire with a vision of change that's beyond any individual to achieve on their own.
- Convince them the other collaborators are essential to the effort and up for the challenge.
- Prevent any one party from benefiting so much from the collaboration that other participants feel their contributions are being exploited.[70]

Consider pulling the group together early on to create a shared experience or activity to help coalesce that sense of community. Help the group identify shared values, and they'll be motivated to come together to achieve the common goal.

Let's return to our cyberattack example. You can imagine how quickly collaborators grasped that they would all need each other to halt a cross-border digital scheme that might have helped Russia succeed in the first European invasion of one country by a neighbor since World War II. Clearly, both government and tech experts would be needed to meet the challenge. The high stakes of the crisis quickly bonded the participants and inspired them to trust each other, with all parties clearly standing to benefit from a positive outcome.

Your collaboration may not be as high-stakes, but the example points up the importance of rapid community building to bond collaborators and get them moving.

## Process

Once you've recruited your collaborators and built a sense of community, you need to create effective processes that will guide the collaboration. When you have a pressing challenge and are convening a group to collaborate, you may feel a sense of urgency to dive in and get to work. This is known as *plunging in*—a common decision bias you want to avoid.

For the collaboration to be successful, everyone involved needs clarity on the group's purpose and the processes you'll use for working together. Remember, you're congregating people from different organizations and corporate cultures. You need everyone to agree on methods so they can collaborate effectively. This begins with a common understanding of why the collaboration is forming and what it hopes to achieve.

To get participants from various organizations working together, you have to create the right conditions, say business-school professors Paul Adler of USC, Charles Heckscher of Rutgers, and Laurence Prusak of Columbia, in their article, "Building a Collaborative Enterprise."[71]

What creates the right context for a successful collaboration? There are several key elements:

- **Define a shared purpose**
- **Cultivate an ethic of contribution** that values advancing that common purpose
- **Develop scalable procedures** for coordinating interdependent effort
- **Create an infrastructure** that values and rewards collaboration

Here's a short synopsis of each.

## Define a shared purpose

To foster healthy collaboration, there should be a shared purpose. Why? Most people are self-interested—in both their personal and professional lives.

To overcome the inclination to focus on the individual, collaboration leaders need to develop a shared purpose. An effective shared purpose will dial the group in on their overarching objectives, how they position themselves relative to partners and competitors, and what contribution they will make to customers and, more broadly, society. To help align the team around the collaboration's purpose, it can be helpful to have participants create a group agreement or charter. See Chapter 7 for more details.

**TWELVE SKILLS**

### *Cultivate an ethic of contribution*

Following on the heels of purpose, the best collaborations focus on their contribution rather than only on their immediate work. Emphasizing contribution over effort engenders a sense of trust and commitment and pushes the group to elevate their investment beyond simply working hard. For example, a focus on effort may emphasize money or hours spent, number of people involved, or other projects you're not working on. Rather, collaborators focus on what their work (and that of others) enabled the team to accomplish, how they solved complex challenges in a new way, or key moments that led to breakthroughs.

### *Develop interdependent processes*

In a large collaboration, subgroups often work interdependently, meaning they work on projects that are separate but connected to one another. Standard process tools such as project planning, process mapping and other formal protocols support the effort, but all this work must be coordinated. Interdependent process management is flexible and adaptive but must function within an overarching framework and appropriate protocols (for example, what each sub-team works on and how). Teams rely on their own efforts but must work diligently to maintain overall alignment. In these environments, clear communication and transparent decision processes are essential to coordination.

## Create collaborative infrastructure

In collaborative efforts, individuals may work on multiple teams and on multiple work streams. This requires an infrastructure that supports this feature. Work distributed and integrated across teams will be managed by team leaders, who must guide and direct the process. In general, this means a matrix structure: People have more than one boss (sometimes called solid-line and dotted-line reporting). For example, a team might report to someone who oversees all aspects of the project in one geography, but it might also report to someone who coordinates across all teams in the same functional area. Collaboration leaders need to make those relationships visible and clear, and to get ongoing feedback about how well the system is working and how individuals are contributing.

## Virtual collaboration

When you bring together people from around the globe, collaboration will almost certainly be virtual (or hybrid). Leaders can organize productive virtual collaboration if they're mindful of how to do so. While technology is essential for collaboration today, rolling out the tech tools is no guarantee of success. To be useful, the chosen technology needs to be universally understood and adopted by all participants. You could chat in Slack, use Trello boards to track progress, and share files through Monday, for example, but beware of tools that might discourage or exclude some participants. Uneven adoption and unofficial or private communication channels may create bottlenecks or choke off information sharing.

Technology is merely a means to an end in your collaboration. It should maximize sharing among all participants. If it's not doing that, it's time to revisit your tech choices. Often, leaders will need to manage multiple tech channels and encourage people to participate in a variety of ways. Different people feel safe and empowered in different spaces, so one tech solution may not fit all.

Good collaborations encourage ideas by getting participants involved in what's being built. You can encourage diverse voices by making sure all participants have a turn to speak, and—even more importantly—each feels acknowledged and heard. Consider how you'll express that recognition in the tech platforms you choose.

By this point, you've defined your purpose, process, and conditions. You've also chosen the tech tools that will enable this collaboration. What's next? Making sure your collaboration fulfills its hoped-for goal of generating breakthrough ideas.

## Performance

Now that you've set up your collaboration, it's time to put actions in motion to get the results you want. The collaboration needs to perform, sparking creative thought and leading to the breakthrough needed. We'll cover the important factors here.

### *Unleashing creativity*

It's the leader's job to inspire everyone to participate in creative thinking. It's why the collaboration was convened—to cross-pollinate ideas from people with different experiences and backgrounds.

When asked to brainstorm, some people will say that they're not creative. We don't think that's true, but some people need more permission and encouragement to take the risk of sharing their wildest notions with their colleagues.

The leader can help by providing tools that inspire new thinking. For instance, ask the group questions such as:

- What if we imagined that all our assumptions about X are wrong?
- What if we looked at the problem in reverse, or from an opposing point of view?
- If you were the CEO, what would you do next?
- Could you list all the pros and cons of these options?

- Can we take the next ten minutes and shout out whatever comes into our heads for a solution? There's no such thing as bad ideas.

- Could you create a mind map of your ideas around this?

Keep challenging your group to break out of established thinking patterns and push past their usual boundaries, to come up with new possibilities.

### *Evaluating performance*

Measuring performance in a collaboration is more challenging than it is measuring individual or in-house team goals. You're striving for major breakthroughs here, with a sizable group of participants across multiple organizations. Gauging success won't be as easy as determining whether sales increased 5% last quarter.

You need to quantify the collaboration's work in measurable ways so you know if you're making progress. Leaders need to manage the collaboration for results, keeping the participants on track and headed toward the goal. Everyone involved needs to understand the outcome you want, and how you will measure and monitor progress along the way.

## Challenges with evaluating collaborations

Over the past several decades, measuring performance has improved greatly, with innovations such as comprehensive scorecards and analytics that enable measuring and evaluating performance across wide swaths of data in detail. Problems in measuring performance persist, such as balancing focus on short- versus long-term objectives, evaluating the right mix of process and outcome metrics, and judging performance at both individual and team levels. Collaborations need to consider and work to offset these difficulties.

## An effective way to measure collaboration performance

In their article "Performance Management Shouldn't Kill Collaboration," researchers Heidi Gardner and Ivan Matviak point out that often focusing on near-term, individual performance undermines the very collaboration that is intended to drive overarching organizational goals.[72] To address this challenge, they recommend a multi-part performance scorecard, with shared goals to focus on strategic targets, while continuing to hold teams and employees accountable for hitting individual results.

In development of the scorecard, each element—for example, collaboration, team, individual—is weighted according to its importance in reaching shared targets.

The proper weighting balances all elements and keeps everyone focused on major outcomes.

---

### EXAMPLE: What successful collaboration looks like

We recently worked with the leadership team of a nonprofit organization that grew through mergers over the years. As a result, separate divisions had different service offerings, staffing models, clients, and funding sources. The leadership team consisted of the CEO, three division heads, the CFO, the HR head, and the quality-assurance lead.

The team was presented with this question: *How would you allocate an unsolicited $1 million gift?* Of course, everyone's first thought was: *Allocate it to my area.* The CFO pointed out the need to avoid a turf war by creating decision-making guidelines for donations, savings, and human resources.

To shake up their thinking, we asked: *If you were the CEO, what criteria would you use to decide, keeping in mind the needs of the organization from top to bottom?* This idea energized the team to think in new ways.

Together, they created a set of allocation guidelines that balanced overall needs with those of departments and individuals. The collaboration was successful because all members were willing to step into this role, imagining themselves in the CEO's chair. They shifted from a self-interested perspective to considering the organization's larger mission.

---

Sometimes a difficult decision isn't financial but about how a direction supports your values, your staff, or the future of your organization. Without guidance from the leader, you can see how easy it is for collaborators to head off in many different directions. With the right guidelines and scorecards in place, you can get to the point of the collaboration: To generate creative breakthroughs.

## Barriers to effective collaboration

It's fun reading about groundbreaking collaborations, but not every collaboration succeeds. Let's think about what prevents productive collaboration.

Some efforts end up with the wrong people. You might have an imbalance between departments or roles such as too many people from sales and not enough from the product division, or vice versa. Perhaps your group didn't include people with all the required skill sets.

In addition, many collaborations fail to create a safe environment. Participants from other countries or with different experience levels, for example, don't contribute their ideas. As a result, the needed cross-pollination that creates breakthrough thinking doesn't take place.

There can be negative incentives that punish collaboration, leading people to give short shrift to the collaboration's work. That's not the only way rewards can go wrong either—sometimes we focus on individual accomplishments instead of on actions that benefit the whole group.

Keep in mind that not every group of people that comes together to tackle a challenge needs to collaborate at a high level. Just because you've assembled more than five people doesn't mean you need to write a charter, build sophisticated processes, and establish game-changing goals. Sometimes a workgroup—a handful of people gathered to solve a problem—is all you need. Think about whether your issue has the scope and challenge level where a collaboration is truly needed.

Your collaboration doesn't have to end up as a dud. Follow the steps highlighted in this chapter to tip the odds of success in your favor.

*Lay your plans for productive collaboration*

As you can see, careful planning underlies successful collaboration. You need to assemble a diverse group of people who are confident enough to share their ideas to people they've just met. They'll look to you to define the collaboration's purpose, to create rewards that keep participants motivated, and to set priorities and guiding principles.

Once that groundwork is laid, you will play a key role in stimulating creativity and encouraging all participants to share their thoughts. If the group hits a dead end, they'll look to you for prompts to get the ideas flowing again.

If your collaboration is successful, a new paradigm will emerge. Something needs to change—across your organization or even across your entire industry. That means it's time for the next step in your leadership journey: Spearheading a successful change initiative, to make sure your great new idea becomes a reality.

## Getting started with effective collaboration

In this chapter you learned our 3P method for becoming an effective collaborator: People, Process, and Performance. You also explored what it takes to set up a collaborative effort, staff it appropriately, drive the process, and reach your outcomes.

When it's time to lead a collaboration, you should be positioned to succeed. Here are some reminders as you start:

- **Set the example.** Establish yourself as someone in your organization who can lead a large-scale collaboration.

- **Staff with the right team.** Be sure to put the right people on the bus, as the saying goes, for maximum representation, diversity, creativity, and drive. Your progress will depend on it.

- **Manage the process.** From setting purpose to managing tasks and activities, the process you use will need to keep the collaboration moving forward and accomplishing real work. That includes effective management of virtual teams.

- **Measure the outcomes.** Performance will depend on having the right metrics at the individual, team, and overall effort levels. Be sure to manage all aspects of performance simultaneously.

Not everything you and your colleagues do day to day will be a major collaboration—that's to be expected. However, when it is time to convene to make a breakthrough, be sure to leverage the points in this chapter—they've been proven to be effective across a wide range of industries and organizations. Using your 3P approach to collaboration, you're not only ready to harness the power of large groups, but you're also prepared to change your organization. That's the topic of the next chapter—leading change.

# 9
# Revamping Change Leadership

There was a time when business consultants like us used to help leaders with change management. It was common for organizations to make an investment in a new process or technology (or both) and, to ensure success, a change in team and individual behavior would be needed. A leader inside the organization would direct the effort to make it happen, often with the assistance of outside change experts. A change of this magnitude might take several months or, in complex cases, years. Getting the change to stick requires a major investment of time and energy.

Organizations still change today, but the difference between contemporary change efforts and those of years past is the persistence. Now change never stops—organizations are in a constant state of flux.

We live in the VUCA era: Change characterized by volatility, uncertainty, complexity, and ambiguity.[73] The pace of business has greatly accelerated owing to effects of globalization, technology, and rapidly evolving customer demands. By the time you execute one change effort, another is already on the horizon.

This feature of change—the constancy—has created both unrest and confusion for employees. In his article "Don't Just Tell Employees Organizational Changes Are Coming—Explain Why," Employee Engagement and Change Manager Morgan Galbraith notes that almost one-third of all US employees surveyed don't understand why the changes affecting them are happening. As he notes, "When employees don't understand why changes are happening, it can be a barrier to driving ownership and commitment and can even result in resistance or push back. And employees' resistance to change is a leading factor for why so many change transformations fail."[74] Change leadership is therefore one of the Twelve Skills.

## Why change leadership?

Leading ongoing, dynamic change defines the workplace today. This isn't only about the content and structure of the work itself, but also employees' reaction to and acceptance of it. Successful leaders must contend with constant change, whether it's something as far-reaching as a pandemic or geopolitical crisis, or simply a strong new competitor. For most leaders working in the middle of the organization, hiring outside help isn't an option. Driving change must be done by themselves. That's what this chapter is about: Helping you learn to effectively lead change with your teams with both positive and lasting effects.

That said, if you've been working for more than a few years, you've been involved in some type of organizational change. Whether that has been simple or complex, you no doubt have both skills and experience under your belt.

## Chapter goals

Change is no longer the exception—it is a constant in the workplace. However, attempting it too quickly, or without considering the direct or collateral effects, often leads to failure. Following a structured process can make the crucial difference to any change effort, large or small.

Using the tools we describe in this chapter, you will be able to:

- Prepare yourself and your team for change
- Implement change initiatives more effectively
- Sustain focus on the change

**TWELVE SKILLS**

---

**EXERCISE: Change leadership—self-assessment**

Before we describe each step in more detail, let's take stock of your current change leadership skills. For each question, rate yourself on a scale of 1 to 5.

| Change leadership—self-assessment | | | | |
|---|---|---|---|---|
| I take the time to communicate changes, why they're needed, and the benefits. | 0 | 1 | 2 | 3 |
| I'm careful to execute the change and monitor progress while diagnosing and responding to obstacles. | 0 | 1 | 2 | 3 |
| I work to institutionalize the new approaches and guard against backsliding. | 0 | 1 | 2 | 3 |
| Total score | | | | |

If your score came to 7 or more, you have good change leadership skills already. If you landed somewhere in the 4-6 range, you're familiar with change leadership but need some additional work. A score or 4 or under, and you'll want to think carefully about both your skill and experience levels. Like the other chapters, that's what you're here for—skill building.

---

# Change leadership defined

Change leadership is a broad concept, so what is it really? According to strategy advisors David Lancefield and Christian Rangen, in their article "4 Actions

## REVAMPING CHANGE LEADERSHIP

Transformational Leaders Take," at the highest level: "Leading change involves helping the organization transcend its current positioning, performance, and capabilities."[75]

This means that the highest levels of change require leadership that pushes teams and organizations to significantly surpass their performance levels. Exceptional, dynamic change leaders continuously anticipate, plan for, and adjust to the ever-changing landscape. In so doing, they guide their teams to performance that significantly exceeds where they are today.

Lancefield and Rangen suggest that to bring empowerment to employees to support change initiatives, leaders need to:

- Describe a clear purpose so employees know what they're aiming for
- Set out expectations for performance, behaviors, and self-care
- Make performance data transparent to everyone
- Give people the tools they need to do their work
- Invest in their development and upskilling—in particular, decision making, new technologies, and creativity
- Give employees genuine autonomy to make decisions
- Listen to—and act on—suggestions[76]

**TWELVE SKILLS**

While these leader behaviors are vital to driving change initiatives, they are also helpful guides to engage the workforce daily.

## Skill builder Nine: PTS change leadership process

How can you effectively lead your organization through successive waves of change? Leaders who successfully lead dynamic change know how to get their team to buy in to the change, monitor and course correct as change is implemented, and make sure the new paradigm persists.

These actions form the basis of our three-step PTS process:

1. **Prepare:** Communicate that change is coming, why it's needed, and its benefits.

2. **Transition:** Execute the change; monitor progress; sense, diagnose, and respond to obstacles.

3. **Sustain:** Institutionalize the new approach and guard against backsliding.

If these steps seem intuitive, excellent. The process to lead change effectively isn't complex; executing it successfully, especially over time, is difficult, however, and worthy of your understanding and practice.

## Change management versus change leadership

You might be wondering if change management is the same as change leadership. Fair question. The answer is no—they are both important and related but different.

Change *management* is oversight of the magnitude, scope, pace, and impact of change. It's the essential monitoring that tells you what's working and what's not. It's the operational side of change. When you think about a project plan and a leader driving the team to milestones and outcomes, that's change management in action. It's managing the changes that need to occur.

Change *leadership* is the strategic or visionary side of change. It's the human side of change that enables the mechanics of change management to occur. The plan created during change management is tied to a purpose and communicated to the team. When obstacles appear or barriers slow the plan, it's the enthusiasm, persuasion, and coalition building that sustains the work and provides a means to overcoming the slowdown. It's more than being a cheerleader, though—you educate team members about the change initiative and show the impact it will have.

Outstanding leaders need to excel at both aspects of driving constant change—the mechanical and the human. Effective change leadership is what's most lacking at many organizations.

## Prepare

Nothing can create more chaos than a leader who—suddenly and without advance notice—announces a major change. It's not uncommon for a leader to read an article about a new management technique and, in a desire to improve their team's performance, implement it forthwith. Take the concept of open-plan offices. There is some research that suggest open-plan offices promote teamwork and enhance idea sharing. A leader might decide to remove cubicles and switch to an open-office layout without first doing research, soliciting staff input, or considering pros and cons.

Unfortunately, a leader who does this may soon be scratching their head, wondering why their seemingly straightforward change initiative backfired. Some workers may quit, because they liked the feeling of privacy and a space they could decorate. Others switch to hybrid work to minimize the change, or transfer to another department that still uses cubicles, or—more likely, in this day and age—avoid coming into the office entirely.

The synergy and enhanced productivity imagined by the leader in this case didn't materialize. A year or two later, the office may transition back to cubicles. Money, time, and energy were wasted because the leader didn't prepare for change. As this simple story demonstrates, the preparation phase is critical to the success of your change plan.

## Build the case for change

When you embark on a change, it's important to explain why it's needed. What's the benefit? What are the implications of not making this change? Before launching a change initiative, smart leaders build a compelling case for why this change needs to happen now. They also explain why it's the best option under the circumstances. Mandating change rarely works. In the era of the knowledge worker, employees need more compelling reasons to change than *The boss says so*.

Sometimes the case for change is made for you. For instance, you must change how you do business because of new supplier mandate. More often however, we choose our change. Organizations enter new markets, decide to divest divisions, or select a new key officer. Regardless of the circumstances, it's essential that the road to change be paved with a compelling reason.

According to Ryan Raffaeli, in his paper "Leading and Managing Change," there are two basic types of organizational change.[77] The first type addresses a *performance gap*—the organization has fallen behind competitors in efficiency and productivity. It's no longer a top performer and, to catch up, its performance needs to improve. The other type capitalizes on an *opportunity gap*—the organization can capitalize on emerging circumstances to stay ahead of competition into the future. Customer preferences are shifting, or the external environment and the chance are present to leapfrog forward. The differences between the two are not so much in the composition but rather in the framing of the change with employees.

### *The emotional side of change*

As you prepare your organization or team for change, don't forget the emotional aspect. It's easy to become focused on timelines, milestones, and measurements, tuning out the people who are affected by the change. Be sure to consider what they are afraid of losing, though. For instance, when many offices closed due to COVID-19 and companies switched to home-based work, leaders were forced to consider the ramifications:

- If we shift to remote work, how will I maintain harmonious working relationships with my colleagues?

- How will my junior staff actually get their work done at home?

- How can I be in the house all day when my kids will be home too?

There was a long list of things people feared when the transition from the workplace started. However, we eventually learned how to work productively at home, managing expectations and demonstrating our progress. We even discovered how to keep up social connections. Now work has permanently changed, with some workers and organizations not returning to the office.

The lesson is simple: If leaders hear workers' concerns and help them manage the worries change brings, workers can often come out the other side with new skills and added confidence.

### Understanding change resistance

If you've ever led a change initiative, you've probably encountered workers who dragged their feet on tasks or even engaged in behaviors that were counter to the change management plan. You may have wondered: *Why are my people so resistant to this change, which will ultimately make their work lives better? I've made a logical case for why they need to change, so why the continued pushback?*

It's easy to see people as simply oppositional or change-phobic, but research has shown there's more to it. Recalcitrant workers often have a competing or conflicting commitment, Harvard professors Robert Kegan and Lisa Laskow Lahy found. In their article "The Real Reason People Won't Change," they note that the person may not be consciously aware of this competing commitment.[78] Behind the competing commitment may be a deep-rooted idea, which the authors dub a *Big Assumption*. It's just an idea, but the person thinks of it as a fact, which keeps them grounded in the current state.

For instance, a team member may have a lifelong fear of failure that traces its origin to some childhood embarrassment. To this day, this person dreads taking on highly challenging assignments that might expose their limitations. While you think you're offering a golden advancement opportunity, they see the change as a threat to their wellbeing and career success.

To overcome a worker's Big Assumption, you first need to diagnose it. Ask questions such as:

- What would you like to change at work, to be more effective?
- If you imagine doing the opposite of the undermining behavior, do you feel discomfort or fear?

- What worrisome outcome are you preventing by engaging in this behavior?
- What are you committed to?
- What are your competing commitments?[79]

These questions should help identify the worker's Big Assumption, after which you can gather performance data, looking for evidence that might contradict their Big Assumption. Then question that assumption, demonstrating that it may not be true.

---

### EXAMPLE: Held to the budget

One of us worked with a leader named Dawn, a senior vice president at a large consulting firm. Senior leadership, including Dawn, had decided that long-term success required a shift in their service offerings. Dawn would need to close down one particular service. No one would lose their job—team members providing this service would shift to other roles.

Despite company-wide agreement that the change was needed, Dawn continued to sell the obsolete service. Frustrated, the CEO called her into his office to question this. Dawn said simply: "Twenty million dollars." "What?" asked the CEO. "I understand we're moving away from this service offering," she replied. "It makes sense. But we sell $20 million of this service every year. Right now, it's March. I asked the finance department to show me revised financials that accurately depict the ramp-down of this service and the increase in the new product line. They say there is no adjustment to the financials."

> The new product had yet to provide any revenue. Dawn was sure she'd be held responsible for the revenue gap until the new service caught on. Her competing commitment was to fulfill her revenue responsibility, no matter what. This dovetailed with her Big Assumption that missing sales targets must be avoided at all costs.
>
> To get Dawn's buy-in, the CEO needed to free her from that revenue responsibility and update the financial forecast. Once assured, Dawn stopped selling the old service.

As our example shows, competing commitments—like Dawn's sense of responsibility for a possible revenue gap—can cause reasonable people to vigorously resist change. For a change to succeed, everyone needs to understand the reason for the change—the real, high-level reason. Nothing gets team members digging in their heels more than being told they need to change what they're doing, period. Spell out what's in it *for them*—how their work lives will be improved. Once everyone's on board, you're ready to start executing your change.

Something to keep in mind here is that you may be better at this than your senior leaders. You may have a better pulse on what matters to the team on the ground. Don't hesitate to jump in and provide this valuable information. It may make the difference between success and failure.

## Transition

Your preparation phase is complete—congrats! Now you're ready to roll out your change initiative. Your team must leave old approaches behind and adopt new ones. This is the tough stuff.

As you execute your change plan, consider these five core practices that Harvard experts identified in *Managing Change: Expert Solutions to Everyday Challenges*. They are:

- **Craft an implementation plan.** Identify all needed steps.

- **Enlist key people.** Get buy-in from team members who can drive the change.

- **Send consistent messages.** Keep reiterating the purpose and mission.

- **Develop enabling structures.** Identify and provide needed resources.

- **Celebrate milestones.** Achievements should be recognized.[80]

Let's look at each of these transition best practices in more depth to unpack helpful strategies.

**TWELVE SKILLS**

## *Craft an implementation plan*

A change plan can be complex, full of detailed action steps and coordination activities. What's really needed, though, is a straightforward approach that breaks down the plan into discrete steps: What needs to happen and when. A good change plan has the following attributes:

- **It's simple.** It shouldn't try to do too much at once. Make it clear, concise, coherent, and easy for team members to understand.

- **It considers input from the affected people.** Don't impose a plan on your team. Make sure they have input to the process. People buy into the things that they help create.

- **It's structured in achievable chunks.** Create milestones along the way, where everyone can see progress.

- **It specifies roles and responsibilities.** Without clarity and accountability for who will do what and when, change won't happen.

- **It's flexible.** Remember, we live in the VUCA world—craft alternatives you can use if needed, as your change initiative plays out.

You need to keep each of these considerations in mind to build a change plan that can be executed.

## *Enlist key people*

Along with a clear change plan, you need to garner support from your team by establishing defined roles and responsibilities in the execution process. You need to determine who is required to do what, on which timeline.

To return to our open-plan office example, that change plan would need to assign roles for who will:

- Manage communication with affected team members
- Arrange for disposal of old cubicles and furniture on move-out day
- Order new open-plan furniture in time for the move-in date
- Find a place to store new furniture if it arrives early
- Hire and oversee the assembly crew
- Book an interim workspace for the team during changeover days
- Organize an event to celebrate the new layout

Tasks that are no one's—or everyone's—responsibility are tasks that don't get done. Brainstorm with team members about all the steps needed to make sure the process is clear, and to be sure that every action has a deadline and a responsible person.

**TWELVE SKILLS**

### *Send consistent messages*

Discontent, speculation, and confusion thrive in the white spaces created by inconsistent communication. Where no information exists, people will create narratives to fill in the gaps. Often this information is inaccurate or incomplete. That's why ongoing, consistent information is so important. Team members should never be in the dark; if they are, be prepared for some strange information to emerge.

Provide updates routinely, brief the team on any plan changes and why they're needed, and make positive examples about team members who've successfully completed their tasks. Remember: It's almost impossible to communicate too much during a change.

As your change rolls out, continue to listen closely to frontline workers—those people who are in touch with how changes are impacting customers. Remember, they see firsthand how your change efforts affect customers. You can be the important linchpin who ensures communication flows up to senior management as well as out to frontline team members

### *Develop enabling structures*

Enabling structures are those activities that lay the foundation for change programs to achieve success. They include things like pilot programs, which give people an opportunity to learn and experiment in controlled ways; training programs that provide people with the skills they need to be effective in their roles; and reward systems that align incentives with the actions to incent the right types of behavior.

Enabling structures instill a sense of direction, responsibility, and ownership for the change at multiple levels in the organization.

## Celebrate milestones

It's a mistake to wait until the end of your change initiative to celebrate your team's success. If you don't provide frequent, positive reinforcement, you won't be able to generate and sustain the momentum needed to see the project through to completion.

Be sure to celebrate all along the way. Think of your transition goals and everything your team accomplishes. It's never too soon to point out who found the best deal on open-plan office furniture or found a cool co-working spot the team could use as a home base during the changeover.

As you think of ways to laud team members, be creative and continuous in your pursuit of things to celebrate. You can even celebrate small mistakes by recasting them as a *learning of the month*. That's why hospitals hold regular morbidity and mortality conferences—learning and improvement are the goal. Team members may be afraid to discuss mistakes, but if you cast the mistakes as a welcome learning opportunity, you'll get more information on how to keep your change plan on track.

Before you declare mission accomplished, confirm that your goals have been met. You don't want to be that person who boasts about your accomplishments, which later turn out to be fleeting.

Bottom line: Don't wait to get to the end of the change initiative to show you're getting results. Make short-term wins visible so team members see for themselves that their hard work is making the change happen.

You've come a long way with your change plan, following the steps to prepare and transition your team into executing the change. There's one final step: You need to make sure your change becomes permanent and doesn't just slowly fade away.

## Sustain

How often have you seen a company make a major change, announce their success, and in short order watch things slip slowly back to the way they were? It's all too common. That's why the final step in our model is so important. You need to sustain the change by making sure it becomes institutionalized as the new organizational standard. Below is a set of strategies to help.

## *Be persistent*

It's easy to pat yourself on the back and become complacent once your change is done. Our advice is simple: Resist the temptation. Always be on guard for reverting to the old way of doing things. Remember, there's often a group of people standing on the sidelines during any change effort, waiting for leadership to move on to their next big idea. As soon as they see attention shifting elsewhere, they backslide into the old way of doing things. An effective change leader doesn't allow this to happen.

We once had a client whose staff would sarcastically refer to change initiatives as the *Idea du Jour* or *The CEO's Book Club*—an initiative launched every time the CEO finished a business book. In this case, it was a warranted reaction—the CEO didn't follow through with implementing these new programs.

Your continued discussion of this change's value and its results sends the message that this wasn't a temporary whim, and staff need to adapt to the new normal.

## *Maintain the climate*

If you've ever visited a major mountain, you may have learned that lofty peaks can create their own microenvironments. Consider Mount Everest, with the world's highest peak at just over 29,000 feet. Weather at the upper altitudes can be vastly different from that below; conditions can even vary on the different sides of the mountain and on nearby peaks. Worse, weather conditions can change drastically within minutes. The rapid emergence of a blizzard in May of 1996 cost eight climbers their lives, in one of the worst climbing accidents of all time. The story of the expedition is now part of a simulation that teaches teams the power and peril of group dynamics and decision making.[81]

As a dynamic change leader, you control the climate around you, shaping the experiences of your colleagues and teams. If you come into the office in a foul mood, it's likely everyone else will soon be in a bad mood too, and that will undermine your change effort. In fact, we once worked with an organization that employed a leader with such dramatic daily mood swings that the company receptionist would email a message to his entire team right after he arrived at work, letting them know if they were in for a sunny or stormy day. That's the impact a leader's mood can have.

You *need* to project an upbeat mood. Even if you've seen setbacks and aren't feeling thrilled about the progress your team is making, keep feelings of disappointment and frustration under control. Be mindful of the fact that somewhere around the office, a team member has checked off a task or reached a milestone. Focus on that achievement, and work quietly behind the scenes to overcome any obstacles.

## Model new behavior

One way you can help institutionalize change is to continually spotlight and celebrate team members who excel at modeling new behaviors and methods. Make their can-do spirit widely known, and as they see for themselves that modeling the right behaviors will get them noticed and rewarded, other employees will soon follow suit.

There are many ways to do this, from a short profile in the company newsletter to an announcement at a meeting. Each mention of how the change is succeeding reinforces that your interest hasn't waned. This also discourages holdout team members from regressing to old habits.

Note that recognition is always great, has a powerful impact, and can be done anytime and anywhere. While they are also beneficial, monetary rewards are often more complicated to plan and administer. It's also possible to discount people's sense of accomplishment with financial rewards they find inappropriately small. Whenever possible, focus on recognition rather than financial rewards.

## Rescue foundering change

Not every change plan goes smoothly. Despite all your efforts, you will no doubt encounter unexpected obstacles on the way. Monitoring your change progress is therefore vital to your long-term success. Close monitoring should clue you in if your change initiative is in trouble and an intervention is needed.

Remember, a change leader's role is to carefully observe, analyze, and understand how the people going through the change *feel* about it. If team members are dragging their feet or are openly oppositional to your plan, they may be being pushed too far too fast, or you may need to adjust aspects of the plan based on new information.

If your change plan hits the rocks, the most important thing is to reset and reinforce the priority. One of our corporate clients was part way through a major change effort when he noticed some senior leaders reverting to previous modes of behavior. When the leader realized this, he called a meeting to get updates from all the leaders on their change efforts and their progress. This simple step of reasserting the leader's commitment was enough to energize the team to get the process back on course.

### *Stay the course*

Somewhere along the journey to completing your change efforts, it is likely the goalposts will start to seem too far away and team members will lose heart. Your role as a change leader is to be on the lookout for this and help your team get over the humps. Be mindful that you can sometimes rally the troops, and other times you should call on senior management to send a motivational message. Remember, you're asking your team to do something hard—to abandon the comfortable status quo in favor of something that will be better in the future. Offer continual encouragement, public recognition for achievers, and congratulations as milestones are hit. It's your job to keep people motivated, even when the going gets tough.

Remember what you learned in the "Understanding change resistance" section above. If needed, use the questions you saw earlier in this chapter to tease out which competing commitment or Big Assumption may be keeping your team from embracing the change. Do your best to work through the issues and to keep everyone on board.

## Getting started with change management

Now that you have all three steps of our PTS process—Prepare, Transition, Sustain—you can see how they work together. Prepare for the shift, transition into execution, and then act to sustain your change over time.

There is one final step to take, and that's to begin the cycle again. If this change is accomplished, what additional positive changes does this new order enable? Your team will need to be able to make changes on an ongoing basis, and you need the grit to continue the effort.

Here are a few thoughts regarding how to make changes stick:

- **Set the example.** If you want to be a great change leader, show that you have the ability to change. Master the process and apply it to your own work.
- **Be enthusiastic.** A positive attitude—even during difficult times—can be contagious. Let those around you know that you're a change cheerleader.
- **Commit to the change.** Let your teams know that once the change begins, there is no chance of going back to the old ways of doing things.

The great Indian leader Mahatma Gandhi is credited with the quote, "Be the change you want to see in the world." While you may not be trying to change the world, you will need to change how your team works from time to time. With the PTS method in mind, it's time to advance to the next skills—ones that you will no doubt need to help manage your change: Persuasion and influence.

# 10
# Increasing Persuasion And Influence

When you hear the words *persuasion* and *influence*, what thoughts pop into your mind? Do you see an image of a pushy car salesperson in a plaid sports coat, trying to get someone to buy a vehicle they don't want? How about a fast-talking politician making an empty campaign promise? Or maybe you think of something a little closer to home, like the time you convinced a busy colleague to join an important project team, or when you pleaded with your son or daughter to clean up their room. Despite the diversity in these examples, they all have one thing in common: Getting other people to do something you want them to do. That's what persuasion and influence are about.

## Why persuasion and influence?

Whether you know it or not, you spend considerable time and effort trying to persuade and influence people around you. At work and at home, in school or in community organizations, people at all levels employ persuasion and influence tactics to get work done. The business world is no exception. In today's flat organizations, leaders routinely need to enlist the support of colleagues, team members, and business partners to achieve their goals. Moreover, because the workplace is less hierarchical than it was even twenty years ago, leaders must increasingly enlist the support of employees who don't work directly for them. The implications are clear: To be effective as a leader, you must master the art of persuasion and influence. To do that, you need to learn to understand, and effectively operate in, the politics of your organization.

If this point makes you uncomfortable, that's OK. Many people, when first introduced to persuasion and influence, and especially politics, react somewhat negatively. They think that getting others to do something is more about disinformation and deception than anything else. That couldn't be further from the truth. The tools of influence and persuasion have nothing to do with trickery at all but rather a good understanding of human nature and social science. Our job is to present the key concepts to you in a useful way in this chapter.

## Chapter goals

The principles of persuasion and influence come into play in all aspects of life. Many of us overlook that the fundamentals of these concepts are a science. They can be learned and should be practiced, and you need to develop the skills.

This chapter will increase your knowledge and inspire you to practice, so you will be able to:

- Understand and navigate politics in your organization
- Persuade others to listen to your ideas
- Use the principles of influence to get others to act

---

**EXERCISE: Increasing persuasion and influence—self-assessment**

We established above that you already use the techniques of influence and persuasion, so the question now is how skilled you are in these areas. Check yourself below to see how well you understand what's required to be a master motivator.

Rate yourself using the following scale:
0: Never, 1: Occasionally, 2: Often, 3: Always

**TWELVE SKILLS**

| Persuasion and influence—self-assessment | | | | |
|---|---|---|---|---|
| I'm comfortable with politics and know how politicking works in my organization. | 0 | 1 | 2 | 3 |
| I know and employ the elements of a persuasive argument when I communicate. | 0 | 1 | 2 | 3 |
| I understand and use influence principles to accomplish what I need to. | 0 | 1 | 2 | 3 |
| **Total score** | | | | |

If you scored 7 or greater, you have strong persuasion and influence skills. If you landed 5 or 6, you have some strengths but probably have a few shortcomings where you can improve. A score of 4 or below means you want to invest time and energy into boosting your persuasion and influence repertoire. Regardless of how you fared, this chapter includes information you'll find valuable as a leader.

## Persuasion and influence defined

Persuasion enables you make a convincing argument. You use persuasion techniques to motivate people when you're communicating with them—in a discussion, during a presentation, or in writing. It's about introducing information in a way that gets people to adopt a point of view or take a suggested action.

Influence doesn't come from making a structured argument. For our purposes, it's a set of social-psychology principles that motivate people to take specific actions.

In this chapter we'll elaborate in a way that makes the concepts easy to understand and, more importantly, use.

## Skill builder Ten: Our 3P framework

How can you exert more power in your organization by drawing on these concepts? From our own teaching and coaching, we've identified three separate but related areas that build your image as an authoritative leader.

This gives a three-part process:

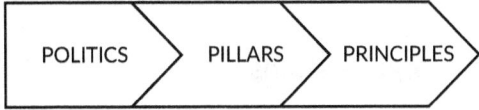

1. **Politics:** Understand the internal political landscape inside your organization—the norms and unseen forces that shape how things get done.

2. **Pillars of persuasion:** Establish the building blocks of constructing a logical, spirited, and

emotional argument that reaches the people you're trying to convince.

3. **Principles of influence:** Recognize the six principles that have been shown to move people to action.

As we delve into the 3P Framework, there are two important things to keep in mind. First, each of the three framework areas is an essential element of your overall ability to sway. Only by understanding and practicing all three will you have maximum impact. Second, to benefit from the content in this chapter, you must both understand and employ the tools—use them or lose them.

Keep in mind that motivating others takes time. Developing skills in each of the three areas requires patience and persistence, but if you put in the work, the rewards will be significant. You'll see.

## Politics in organizations

You might be saying to yourself, *Wait a minute. This chapter is supposed to be about persuasion and influence. Why are we talking about politics?* Good question. It's tempting to think about persuasion and influence independently of each other—both practices do work by themselves. Because you work within an organization, though, you need a solid understanding of the context where you will exercise persuasion and influence. You therefore need to think about organizational politics.

When we ask our clients and students what they think about organizational politics, many of them wince. However, when we ask if they know someone who excels at office politics, we get more positive responses. Many will tell a story of a colleague who always says just the right thing and often knows, ahead of any formal announcement, about changes afoot at the company. Some people admit they admire these coworkers, without realizing they're appreciating political skills for what they are—a requirement for upward movement in a company.

A major reason many people claim to hate politics is that they misunderstand the term and what it means to be political. People think of craven leaders with questionable motives advancing their own interests at everyone else's expense. However, politics is simply how power, authority, and decision-making play out, often in ways that are invisible to the untrained eye. Politics is about understanding the complexities and nuances of how people interact so that you can constructively engage with them in productive, collaborative ways.

To exert influence, it's essential to understand and capitalize on your organization's politics. If you can't skillfully navigate your workplace, you can't influence people. To be politically savvy, you need to know who has power and authority. Who can make important decisions and get things done? Who controls essential resources? Who has critical information and can share it early on? Seen from this angle, politics is simply about understanding what's happening, who is behind it, and how it will ultimately affect you and your team.

### *Building political proficiency*

How can you become more politically savvy? There are a few things you can do, according to Kathleen Kelley Reardon, organizational politics expert. In her article, "Office Politics isn't Something You Can Sit Out," she suggests that leaders first and foremost make an effort to learn about politics and how they play out in their organizations. She highlights five ways:

- **Read about workplace politics and observe those who are skilled at it.** As we stated at the start of this chapter, most people can identify someone in their organization who is skilled politically. Study what they do, emulate some of their behaviors, and study up on what's required to be politically effective in organizations.

- **Try tweaking how and when you say things.** If you're someone that typically defers to other, more vocal colleagues in meetings, take steps to be more assertive. If someone tries to take credit for an idea of yours, say something like, "Yes, I mentioned that option before—I'll expand on my thoughts a bit more now."

- **Consider to whom you're giving power and alter if it's not getting you anywhere.** If you've cultivated relationships with colleagues—even those that help you in your work—but are finding there's no progress, seek out other people or another way.

- **Break out of dysfunctional patterns.** If you have a habit of taking on low-visibility, low-value projects, routinely let people cut you off or talk over you in meetings, or if you never make it a point to connect with senior leaders at your company, it's a good time to change your behavior.

- **Be less predictable.** Predictability is the kiss of death in political organizations. If you're someone everyone knows will do whatever it takes to please people, you set yourself up for being taken advantage of and put yourself at the mercy of those who can use you to advance their own personal agendas.[82]

Like it or not, politics is a fact of life in most organizations. Actively engage in the game, or you may find yourself on the short end of the stick when a major change such as a layoff occurs.

Now we've discussed the basics of how to play, we turn to the two key tools you will use to get help from others: Persuasion and influence.

## Pillars of persuasion

We like the term *pillar* when it comes to persuasion because it conjures up images like the Parthenon in Athens or the Pantheon in Rome. Both images are fitting because, according to Carmine Gallo, an instructor at Harvard University, the "art of persuasion hasn't changed in 2,000 years."[83]

We mentioned persuasion briefly in Chapter 4 on developing clear messaging, but we're going deeper here because it goes beyond just what you say. Persuasion is about shaping how you come across to others in *all* aspects of your interactions with them. At its core, effective persuasion comes from:

1. **Ethos (character):** A person's mental and moral qualities

2. **Logos (logic):** The degree to which an argument adheres to sound reasoning and validity

3. **Pathos (connection):** The emotional connection the audience has to the message

Leveraging these three pillars may sound simple, but it can be hard in practice to weave them all deftly together. Let's outline what you can do to bolster your effectiveness for each.

## *Demonstrating character*

When you engage with others, either formally or informally, are you credible? Do your colleagues believe what you are telling them? Are you seen as knowledgeable and experienced in your work? Have you proven yourself to be honest, and can people rely on you to do what you say you will? If you've answered *yes* to these questions, you are someone who demonstrates a common proxy for character: Credibility.

Credibility has two elements: Expertise and trust. When your colleagues assess your credibility, they examine these two underlying elements, as we did with the questions above:

1. **Expertise:** This is the knowledge, skills, and abilities necessary to accomplish your work. While there are degrees of expertise, most people will conclude you're either competent at your job or not. That boils down to your knowledge level, your skills, and your overall attitude.

2. **Trust:** This is the belief people have in your reliability as well as your integrity. It's the sense that you will follow through on your commitments and do so in a way that is honest and forthright.

If leaders can't be trusted or if they lack the needed skills for their position, they will have a difficult time persuading people to act.

**TWELVE SKILLS**

*Using logic*

Being a person of character and credibility is an essential element of persuasion. If your argument doesn't make sense because it's based on flawed assumptions or a faulty premise with flimsy support, you will likely fail to persuade others. To make a rock-solid case, you need to ground your argument in logical thinking, supported with factual data.

Thanks to advances in data management and analysis, modern organizations often have ample evidence on which to make decisions and act. The expectation that follows is that leaders, at all levels, will take the time to construct thoughtful business cases based on relevant information.

That means that whenever you make an argument—say, for developing a new product or entering an adjacent market—the strength of your claim will be based on the soundness of your reasoning. Your conclusions need to follow on from your beliefs, with sufficient evidence to support what you are asserting. Your audience will need you to walk them through each element of your argument in a way that helps them arrive at the same conclusion as you. If they're not able to do that, or if they find flaws in your conclusion, you will lose the ability to persuade.

As you make your case, be sure not to let your audience get distracted by their own questions. Instead, answer those question, anticipating them where you can. Draw on facts and evidence from your analysis and experience. A compelling, logical argument goes a long way toward winning over those who are ambivalent or opposed. Remember to keep your level of detail or technical information at your audience's level.

It's also helpful to think ahead and deliberately bring up opposing points of view. Skeptics will no doubt challenge you, so be sure to prepare in advance for the kinds of challenges others will raise.

### *Appealing to your audience*

You'd think that a person with high credibility and an airtight argument would be enough to win over any audience, but that's not necessarily true. Very credible and logical people can still come off as unconvincing.

How is that possible? The answer is simple: Those people fail to *understand* their audience. Whether you're talking to two people or a crowd of 222, it's essential to:

- Think through who will be in your audience
- Gauge their interest level and needs
- Craft your message to connect on the points they are interested in hearing

**TWELVE SKILLS**

Truth is, audience members come into every situation with different assumptions, levels of information, values, and priorities. If you depend solely on your message's credibility and logic, you may not resonate with people who need to feel an emotional connection. A highly technical presentation may go over the heads of colleagues without a scientific background. A discussion that fails to mention the costs involved or the anticipated return on investment may turn finance people off. Similarly, a message that doesn't address the people aspects of a proposed initiative may rankle the human resources team.

If you speak to the audience's hot-button issues—no matter how unfounded they may be—they will feel their concerns have been addressed and be more receptive of the overall message. Consider what the majority of people in your audience stand to gain or lose from your proposal. This enables you to build a case that gains support from your proponents while minimizing resistance from potential detractors.

Beyond knowing your audience's different perspectives, you should also know who has what level of authority and who has which role. Think back to our comments on politics: How does your organization make decisions, and who are the important people to consider? There are usually three major groups: Decision makers, influencers, and stakeholders. Decision makers have the ultimate say. Influencers may not have authority, but they have a say and will influence decision makers. There are also stakeholders, who will be impacted by your proposal; although they don't make the decision, the fact they will be affected gives them a voice and some influence.

## Principles of influence

Many of us believe we're too smart to have our opinions swayed by outside influences. How could something as trite as a letter containing a nickel taped to a sheet of return address labels really motivate anyone to make a charitable donation? Can being handed a piece of chicken on a toothpick outside a restaurant entice you to eat there? Don't fool yourself—these tactics aren't purely gimmicks.

Because these methods *do* work, they're commonly used in marketing methods and sales approaches. Even if we're unaware of them, influence techniques are used on us many times every day, spurring us to act without even realizing it. Those people who influence others use these principles with minimal effort and maximal success. Your goal is to learn them and add them to your leadership toolkit.

In his article titled "The Uses (and Abuses) of Influence,"[84] the modern-day father of the science of influence, Arizona State University professor Robert Cialdini, shared the six influence principles he identified in an interview with HBR executive editor Sarah Cliffe. Cialdini's principles are reciprocity, liking, social proof, commitment and consistency, scarcity, and authority. We'll elaborate on them in this section.

## *Reciprocity*

The first, most basic principle of influence is reciprocity: The mutual exchange of benefits or privileges between two parties. Reciprocity is a cultural norm—it's a lesson we learn early in life and one we generally adhere to, regardless of the setting.

The concept of reciprocity is simple. If a person does something kind for us, such as giving us a gift, it creates an expectation that we will return the gesture. Think about the last time you were invited to someone's home for a dinner party. Did you bring something for the host, such as a bottle of wine or a bouquet of flowers? If you did, you engaged in the process of reciprocity—because you were invited for dinner, you felt obligated to return the favor.

Reciprocity is a process of obligation creation and the subsequent fulfillment of the obligation. By doing or giving something to someone, you create a psychological obligation that the other person will feel compelled to repay. The value of the exchange isn't as important as the *expectation* that a gift or favor will be returned. The creation of an obligation is what makes reciprocity such a powerful influence tactic and so powerful in marketing.

How can reciprocity benefit you as a leader? Think of the things you do for people at work as a kind of social savings account. If you help someone out with a challenging problem or make a useful network connection for them, they'll be willing to return the investment when you need help. The more deposits you make with coworkers, the more social savings you can leverage when you need help later.

## Liking

Perhaps the most overlooked principle of influence is liking. Few people ever ask themselves if they're liked by colleagues or, more importantly, how they might become more likable. Some managers tend to think that being liked doesn't matter so long as work is getting accomplished. Don't believe it. Leaders who are liked have a much easier time getting people to help them out when there's a tough task at hand.

Believe it or not, it's easy to increase your likability. One proven way is to spruce up your appearance. If you take the time to pay extra attention to your grooming, refresh your wardrobe, and add a little panache to your style, people will notice and appreciate it. There's an old saying, *The clothes make the man* (and woman too, we assume). What's interesting about the idiom is its twofold power. First, improving how you look *will* get you noticed by the people you work with. Second, upgrading how you look can boost your self-confidence—you'll like yourself even more. It's a win all around.

Another way to grow your likability is to act toward people in kind and considerate ways. Ask yourself when you last complimented someone you worked with. If you can't recall, you can make progress by simply turning up the dial on compliments. We're not talking about phony flattery here; we mean sincere compliments that are both appropriate for the workplace and give your colleagues a sense of your genuine appreciation for them. It's not hard to tell someone they're doing a great job, or that you admire how they look at challenges through a positive lens. Who doesn't want to hear that?

There are other ways to enhance your likability, such as connecting with people through a shared experience or passion. Connecting strengthens the bonds of camaraderie. Along with topping up your appearance and giving compliments, connection is part of a powerful triad of behaviors that will improve your likability.

### *Social proof*

What do you do when you need to make a decision but don't have time for in-depth research? Let's say you want to try a new restaurant. We'll bet you quickly check Zagat's ratings, or reviews on Yelp or TripAdvisor, to see what other people think. This is social proof in action.

Social proof is evidence from other people that you should trust a restaurant, a TV show, a behavior—

almost anything. If a restaurant has hundreds of five-star customer reviews, you feel more confident going there than to a restaurant with only four-star ratings.

Social media has redefined the world of social proof. With a web search and a few clicks, we can access immense amounts of information to inform our decision making. It's a quick way of getting answers we feel comfortable with, thanks to the work of others. Social proof is tangible and makes our decisions and our lives easier.

Social proof in the work context is about evidence that you are a leader that others will respect and follow. This can take many forms, including evidence of your likability or credibility, as we've just mentioned; or of your consistency, scarcity, and authority, as we'll discuss next. More formally, you can complete an educational program that provides proof of your skills such as a certificate or a diploma. Professional certifications are another way to give yourself added credibility. You can also work on high-profile projects or volunteer for a committee steering a major change in your organization. All of these will give you visible credibility that you can leverage as a leader.

### *Commitment and consistency*

Has anyone ever told you that's it important to keep your promises, or that actions speak louder than words? If so, then you understand that people strive

**TWELVE SKILLS**

to keep their commitments and demonstrate consistency in their thoughts and deeds.

If you're both consistent and committed, you will earn the reputation as a person who will follow through on your agreements, regardless of circumstances. If you're not sure that's the case, you probably have some work to do. The good news is that you can improve your commitment level—and other people's confidence that you will live up to your word—by making a few behavior changes.

Renowned management thinker Stephen R. Covey, author of the best-selling book, *The 7 Habits of Highly Effective People*, mastered commitment and consistency.[85] In his article "Stephen R. Covey Taught Me Not to Be Like Him," Greg McKeown tells the story of how Covey lived his principle of "be a light, not a critic."[86] While at a dinner party, other guests started criticizing Governor Bill Clinton who, at the time, was running for president. When asked for his opinion, Covey replied that he didn't want to criticize the candidate, adding that if Clinton ever asked him for help, he didn't want to be a hypocrite. Shortly after becoming president, Clinton did call Covey, asking him to come to Camp David to share his teaching with both the President and the First Lady. This story is an excellent illustration of both commitment to a belief and consistency to one's actions.

As a leader, do your beliefs and words align with your actions? Do you demonstrate coherence in your thinking, speaking, and doing? If what you do and what you say are at odds, you will lose credibility as a leader and your ability to influence will be diminished. Take steps to make sure you walk your talk, both professionally and personally.

## Scarcity

*Act now—supplies are limited* is a phrase that no self-respecting infomercial producer would ever leave out of an ad. Why? Given our society's collective FOMO—fear of missing out—savvy marketers know that we place a premium on things in high demand or low supply, or at least that seem to be. As much as we chuckle at the *Call now!* tactic, there is a part of our psyche that whispers, *Maybe we should place an order, just in case.*

Scarcity means there might not be enough to go around, and it often makes people act to avoid losing out. Research shows that people will go to great lengths to avoid loss because, for many, the pain stemming from loss outweighs the pleasure from gains. This behavior is known as *loss aversion,* and it drives a real response from people. You might remember how difficult it was to get toilet paper early in the COVID-19 pandemic, because (largely unfounded) persistent fears of scarcity drove consumers everywhere to buy and hoard it. Fear of loss of toilet paper is a powerful motivator.

How does scarcity affect a leader's influence? You have greater impact on those around you if you build scarcity thinking into your work. Take, for example, your schedule. If you're always available to work on projects or never say no to requests, you create the perception that you always have time to spare. What kind of people have time to spare? People who aren't good at their jobs, because if they were good at their jobs, they wouldn't have time to spare. Think about it. When it comes to your schedule, make sure you guard your availability and manage others' perceptions of it. You want your colleagues to know that your time is limited because you have so many important things you are working on.

## *Authority*

When people don't have time to unpack complicated topics or engage in lengthy research, they default to experts. Experts have comprehensive knowledge in specific areas such as management or medicine. They are authorities in their fields, and people generally defer to the opinion or guidance of those in authority positions.

---

**EXAMPLE: Forget Harvard?**

Have we mentioned that we're executive coaches certified by the International Coaching Federation, and that we belong to the Institute of Coaching at McLean, a Harvard Medical School Affiliate? Did we tell you that we're instructors at Harvard University on the Faculty of Arts and Sciences? Have you figured out that all the content in *Twelve Skills* is drawn from Harvard Business Publishing? Many people consider Harvard and Harvard Business School to be authorities in the fields of business, management, and leadership, which is why we feature it so prominently. We trust all these references give you comfort that we know what we're talking about, that we can teach it, and that our sources of information are highly credible.

---

How can you build your authority? Perhaps you can develop specialized knowledge within your organization and brand yourself as the go-to person for specific topics. You could focus on mentoring and developing junior colleagues and earn the reputation as a talent magnet. You might also get involved in an industry association or a trade group, taking on a leadership position outside your own company, or you could earn a specialized degree or credential. There are many ways to bolster your authority if you're committed to doing so. Also, remember to tell people your credentials (as we did at the start of this section), or they won't know where your expertise lies.

## Getting started with persuasion and influence

At this point you've delved into our 3P model for persuasion and influence: Politics, Pillars of persuasion, and Principles of influence. You've also gained a sense of how the three work together to nudge your contemporaries toward your way of thinking. To enjoy success from these practices, be sure to:

- **Overcome your fears.** It's not uncommon for people to worry about working with these concepts. You need to get comfortable putting them to work.
- **Practice.** These are use-or-lose skills, so find opportunities to apply them, to begin reaping the benefits of improved influence.
- **Be positive.** The approaches generally work for both good and ill purposes. Use them for good.

With persuasion and influence under your belt, you're ready to start pulling all the previous skills together to do what all leaders must do: Execute. That's what's up next.

# 11
# Driving Focused Execution

One of the most vital skills for any leader is their ability to deliver results. If we said that getting results is the *primary* purpose of leadership, we'd be in good company. Researchers Dave Ulrich, Jack Zenger, and Norm Smallwood claim that in their book, *Results-Based Leadership*.[87] All the skills we've discussed to this point will be of little value if you and your team fail to generate results that contribute meaningfully to your organization's goals.

Simply planning and hoping for great results won't get you there. As a manager, you're primarily evaluated on how much you get done, not on how much you plan to do. While important, it's not enough to set high-level goals and then work like crazy to get there. You may have got an A for effort in school, but you won't at work—high grades are reserved for those leaders that achieved what they set out to do. The most effective leaders know a methodical, targeted approach, based on a set of activities that they know will predictably get results, is the only way to work. That's where focused execution comes into play, and that's what we'll cover in this chapter.

## Why execution?

From research and our own coaching, we know that executing well over time is challenging. It takes forethought to figure out what to do, while avoiding those things that only serve as distractions. Discipline is needed to maintain focus—your team's and your own—on your most important priorities. It requires courage to say no to opportunities and mandates that pull you away from essential goals. Execution isn't only about what you choose to do—it's just as much about what you chose *not* to do. Layer over those distinctions a strategic and operational focus, and a short- and long-term horizon, and it should seem clear that executing effectively requires the management of many competing tensions.

The reality is this: There are few leaders that manage these tradeoffs well. In their article "How to Excel at Both Strategy and Execution," consultants Paul Leinwand and Joachim Rotering note that only 8% of leaders excel at both strategy and execution.[88] That statistic alone should give you sufficient desire to focus your efforts on upping your execution game—doing so will give you a leg up on getting ahead at work.

## Chapter goals

Strategy execution is not for the faint of heart. It requires teamwork, discipline, and transparency. You will often need to confront difficult tradeoffs, but achieving results is the point, so it is time to learn.

Using the tools that we describe in this chapter, you will be able to:

- Map out your objectives for execution in a performance model
- Manage (and eliminate) projects, to align with strategic goals
- Measure progress in execution
- Make decisions more rapidly and effectively

---

**EXERCISE: Focused execution—self-assessment**

Are you one of the 8% of leaders who are able to manage both strategy and execution? Let's take a few moments to find out. Assess yourself on each of the following execution-focused questions.

Rate yourself using the following scale:
0: Never, 1: Occasionally, 2: Often, 3: Always

| Focused execution—self-assessment | | | | |
|---|---|---|---|---|
| My team has a model or map of our strategic priorities, which depicts how we create value for our customers. | 0 | 1 | 2 | 3 |
| We manage a focused set of projects that drive progress toward our most important objectives. | 0 | 1 | 2 | 3 |
| We measure progress on both completion of our projects and achievement of our targets. | 0 | 1 | 2 | 3 |
| We periodically assess how well we're doing in meeting our strategic priorities; and when we're not, we recalibrate our actions accordingly. | 0 | 1 | 2 | 3 |
| **Total score** | | | | |

When you tallied your score, did you achieve a 9 or greater? If yes, well done—you have a strong focus on setting goals and driving achievement of them. If you rated yourself in the 6–8 area, you have some areas where you likely excel, but a few changes could make improvements. If you scored 5 or below you have a significant opportunity to hone your execution skills. In this chapter we will give you a process to do just that.

# Execution defined

Before we go any further, let's define execution. We like Catherine Cote's recent definition in her article "5 Keys to Successful Strategy Execution": "Strategy execution is the implementation of a strategic plan in an effort to reach organizational goals. It comprises the daily structures, systems, and operational goals that set your team up for success."[89]

While that sounds straightforward, it's hard to accomplish. Developing a plan is one thing, but the key activity is setting up the structures, systems, routines, and practices to implement it. Years of research has shown that the success rate of execution is low for most organizations. In their book *Profit from the Core*, consultants Chris Zook and James Allen found that between 1988 and 1998, seven out of eight companies in a global sample of 1,854 large corporations failed to achieve profitable growth.[90] They grew profits and revenues by less than 5.5% over that period and failed to earn back their cost of capital. The spoils are great for both organizations and leaders who master execution.

## Skill builder Eleven: The 4M execution process

You might be wondering how in the world you can overcome odds like these when it comes to execution. Well, there is a way.

We've distilled the process of driving effective execution down to four simple steps, which, if followed consistently, will improve your chances at execution:

1. **Model performance:** Create a visual map of your organization's key objectives and performance levels, and how they fit together to create value for your customers.

2. **Manage projects:** Identify all projects, making sure they align with strategy and have strong oversight.

3. **Measure progress:** Constantly measure progress toward completing projects and meeting key targets.

4. **Make decisions:** Hold review meetings to examine if and how course correction will need to be made to ensure you reach your key objectives.

Together, these four steps make up a virtuous cycle of execution that will drive the results you need to achieve as a leader.

Now that you know your strengths and weaknesses in execution and what you need to do at a high level, let's look at each of these steps in depth. We've distilled a set of useful techniques that will help you improve.

## Model performance

You've probably heard the saying, *A picture is worth a thousand words*. One of the best ways to communicate your key priorities as a leader is by creating a visual mapping of your objectives. If you're planning a trip, what would be easier to follow: A good-looking map of where you plan to go, or a lengthy, written document that describes each step of the journey? Most people choose the map. Drawing a map—or modeling your performance, as we call it—will make it easier for your team to understand and see the key relationships among all your highest priorities and internalize how the company (or your department or team) creates value for its customers. You can also see the connections between different departments, initiatives, and projects. That allows workers to see how they contribute to the organization's success—ideally on a single sheet.

### *Show your business model*

Your visual model should illustrate the theory behind your business. It tells the story of how your business creates value for your customers. For-profit and even nonprofit businesses can do this.

Every business's profit model is different. For example, how Facebook makes money (ads on its social platforms) is different from how Target makes money (retail sales of physical products). The model can also show how an organization like the American Diabetes Association meets the needs of its members while working to conquer the disease.

The model of performance helps people understand the underlying activities that create your ultimate value.

*Popular performance models*

You may be wondering what a performance model looks like and how to create yours. There are several well-known models.

An early example is the Activity System Map that Professor Michael Porter presents in his seminal article, "What is Strategy?"[91] The Activity System Map shows how activities fit together to create a company's overall competitive advantage. Any business department or function comprises a set of activities that create value for customers. In the article's example, you can see how the retailer Gap creates value through a unique set of activities that fit together as a system.

A more sophisticated performance model is the strategy map by Robert Kaplan and David Norton in their article, "Having Trouble with Your Strategy? Then Map It."[92] Their model includes four perspectives on value creation: The financial perspective, the customer's viewpoint, an internal view, and a learning perspective. Each of these perspectives can be used in any part of the organization to show how its objectives work together to achieve results.

Today, one of the most popular performance models is the *business model canvas*. Created by Alexander Osterwalder in 2005 and discussed in his 2013 article, "A Better Way to Think About Your Business Model," the canvas organizes nine building blocks on one page to help organizations, both large and small, think holistically about how they deliver on their value proposition.

| Key Partners | Key Activities | Value Propositions | Customer Relationships | Customer Segments |
|---|---|---|---|---|
|  | Key Resources |  | Channels |  |
| Cost Structure |  |  | Revenue Streams |  |

*Business model canvas*[93]

Look at the various performance models. See which one lends itself best to your organization's business strategy and key objectives. Choose the one that best depicts how you and your team create value. Keep in mind that some people work in a cost center where cost reduction is all they focus on. However, it is just as important that support divisions understand how they support the overall strategy and the ultimate customer.

### *Identify and map objectives*

Once you've chosen a performance model, it's time to identify your objectives and either list or draw them inside the model. In each of the models we've discussed, you can organize your key objectives, which represent your highest priorities, in a way that shows how they relate to one another. The sum of your objectives represents your system of performance—the set of priorities that you need to focus on. Be sure that all of your objectives relate to one another in a logical way.

It's one of the toughest things in business, but to become an effective executor, you need to prune out objectives that aren't among your highest priority. Focus on too many objectives and you'll spread your limited resources (for example, time and money) too thinly and accomplish little. To make sure you don't do this, next we'll look at how you manage the projects in your performance model.

## Manage projects

High-performing managers don't spend their day putting out fires, or at least, they try hard not to. They're laser-focused on tasks that help complete their highest-level objectives. These are known as *strategic projects*. Unfortunately, many projects aren't well thought out, don't align with strategic objectives, or are poorly managed. To execute effectively, you have to join that elite corps of leaders who manage projects successfully. Three major areas are essential: People, processes, and communication. In this section we'll walk you through how to prioritize projects and build good project-management skills.

## *The importance of strategic projects*

Why do managers work on projects (or as they are sometimes called, initiatives)? We can't emphasize enough: The point is to focus your energy on achieving your company's highest priorities. Without well-defined projects, it's easy to fritter away time and energy on low-level actions. If you're not careful, you can bite off initiatives that don't accomplish your main objectives—the ones shown in your performance model.

At most companies, the problem isn't that there are no defined projects—rather there are too many. A few years ago, a client of ours at a global organization started a project to—you guessed it—count projects. They stopped after finding 6,000 and focused their efforts on *killing* projects instead.

For some reason, managers believe that, when it comes to execution, more is better—if two projects are good, four must be twice as good. It's not true, though; normally, less is more. For you to be effective as a leader, your goal needs to be to set and work on a narrow set of initiatives—the ones that drive real progress—and stick to them until they're complete. Only then should you pick others to add. This is a major challenge for managers today—too often, there are simply too many projects in the hopper, leading to confusion about priorities.

Strategic projects are so called because they're supposed to move the strategy forward. Any projects that don't should be canceled or put on the back burner. That's easier said than done, though. Effective leaders know better than to keep irrelevant projects alive. Instead, they identify core strategic projects and prune off the rest.

### Capture strategic projects: The benefits focus

Obviously, you can't prioritize your projects if you can't identify them. The first step to better management and execution of projects is to compile a list of all the projects in your purview, after which you can scan for obsolete projects to cut. You should know *why* you're doing each one. Ask yourself and your team:

- How does this project serve the objectives in our performance model?
- What will be better if it succeeds—will costs be reduced, more customers gained?

Seek clarity on intended outcomes and be sure they align with the strategy.

Another question to consider: Are all our initiatives doable? It's surprisingly common to have projects that can't be completed due to lack of resources. If you don't have financial support, technology enablement infrastructure, or just plain staff time to accomplish a project, don't start it. You can test your projects by aligning them to your performance model. If you see projects that don't tie into any objective, they need to go.

Also, be on the lookout for objectives that have no projects. A goal of entering a new market won't succeed unless there are related projects—perhaps market research on customer segments, or developing a marketing plan for a new audience. If all your projects are aligned with your strategy and all your objectives have projects, you'll have made major progress toward improved execution.

### *Dynamic project management*

Despite your best efforts to set consistent priorities and manage your top projects, things will change. The world is simply too complex and fast moving for any organization to remain static. Your priorities and your projects may have to evolve with the marketplace. Think about how quickly companies must change during a financial, supply-chain, or health crisis.

One way to manage projects dynamically is to think about them in total, like a portfolio. All your projects should work in concert to accomplish your strategy. While they are all important, some may increase in priority over time, while others take a back seat. As difficult as it may feel, some may have to be stopped. When you group your projects—for example, by operations-focused projects or strategic ones, or high-risk projects versus low-risk ones—thinking of your array of projects like a stock portfolio will be highly beneficial. You will then have a holistic perspective on your work.

### Measure progress

By this point, you've created a visual performance model, capturing your portfolio of projects and aligning them to the model. Next you want to start measuring how your projects are progressing and gauge how close you are to achieving your group's objectives (or how far you are from that point). That will require you to measure your projects as well as your performance objectives. This section will give you strategies for both.

First, let's understand what a measure is. Simply put: A measure is anything that quantifies the efficiency or the effectiveness of an action. What we like about this definition is that it applies to projects and performance objectives successively. You need to measure projects to make sure you are reaching your milestones; that's efficiency. In terms of your performance objectives, you want to determine whether your projects—individually and in total—are helping you reach your performance goals; that's effectiveness. Ultimately, you need a balance of measures—efficiency and effectiveness, near-term and long-term, leading and lagging—to have a comprehensive view of progress.

A measure provides a quantifiable indicator of whether you're making progress toward your performance objective. Often, you or your organization will use key performance indicators (KPIs) to determine if you are getting closer to achieving your goals, whether they are operational or strategic. Without measurement, projects quietly fail. If no one is checking progress against milestones, no one will notice that the project is behind schedule or has encountered an unexpected obstacle. This is a common area where execution unravels.

---

**EXAMPLE: Out of sight, out of mind**

We both worked on a strategy project at a large government organization, which, as part of the effort, created a list of top initiatives intended to reshape the future of the entity. For years after our work with that client ended, the leaders kept the same list of high-priority initiatives, virtually unchanged.

One day, on a visit to the organization, we asked one of the top lieutenants why none of the strategic initiatives ever came off the list. As he thought about it, he couldn't explain.

Shortly thereafter, senior leaders began reviewing each priority initiative monthly, to ensure they were not just being worked on but were getting finished.

---

## *Set targets*

To effectively measure your progress, you need to know where you're going. Ask yourself questions such as:

- How many new customers do we need to find?
- How much shorter do we want customer hold times to be?
- When do key milestones need to be reached?

Only with defined targets can you tell how much progress you're making toward your goal, whether it be project- or performance objective-based. Without targets, goals will be squishy. It's hard to give clear direction to your team when you're not clear on how far you've come or how much further you need to go. There is nothing as motivating as seeing real progress, but you need targets to make that a reality.

Without targets, your team won't know how high the bar is. Targets help you as a leader determine the level of effort needed to reach your milestone or your objective. Set a target too low, and you'll underperform; set it too high, and you'll demotivate your team. Target setting requires careful thought and consideration on your part. Quantifying targets is also important in part, because you can't do everything at once. Setting precise targets helps you see what's doable with existing resources, and what might need to wait.

There are two things to consider when setting targets. One is the reference point that you use to set each target. For example, is last year's performance plus some improvement amount realistic, or is benchmarking off competitor performance more realistic? Is there an overall business goal you need to contribute to, such as an across-the-board expense reduction? There are different ways to pick reference points, but all targets need them.

The second is engaging your team in the process. People tend to accept those things they are involved in. To engage your team in the target-setting process, at least spend time explaining the logic underlying the targets; being more included will make your team members more on board with the targets. Executing strategy is a team sport, so be sure to engage your team in all aspects of it, especially in capturing data.

### *Capture data*

Finally, to measure progress, you need data—the information, figures, and tools that help you analyze those numbers. For instance, if you say your goal is to improve website traffic by 30%, but you don't know how to use Google Analytics to see visitor trends and traffic sources, you won't know if your initiatives are working. If you need to select new tracking tools, try to do it quickly and move forward—don't get stuck in analysis paralysis.

Once you have the data you need to manage projects and measure your objectives via KPIs and targets, get moving. Although measurement is important, execution is about acting, not just evaluation.

Keep in mind: One of the challenges with measures is that they can cause confusion. Measures are not goals on their own. From our definition above, you'll recall that they are the *quantification* of action. A simple example is as follows.

1. **Performance objective:** Lose weight
2. **KPI or measure:** Weight lost in pounds
3. **Target:** 10 pounds
4. **Project:** Exercise for thirty minutes four times per week

Note that these are separate points, but they work together. The objective is to lose weight. The KPI is weight lost in pounds. The target is 10 pounds. The project intended to drive progress is to exercise for thirty minutes four times a week.

Your progress in exercising four times per week should help you make progress toward your overall objective of losing 40 pounds.

Your weekly measurement might tell you that you've lost three pounds in two weeks—real progress!

That's what a good measure does: It gauges your progress and lets you know where you stand.

## Another important use for measures

So far we've suggested you use measures to help you track progress on your projects and determine if you're getting closer to achieving the objectives in your performance model. It's essential that you do these to execute tactically well. There's also another way to use these two measurement approaches in harmony: To test the success of your strategy overall. Regardless of the day-to-day work you do, ultimately you're concerned with whether the strategy you outlined in your performance model is coming to fruition over time.

Your strategy—the objectives, the projects in your portfolio, and your measures with connected targets—represents a hypothesis. At the time you create it, your strategy is really your best estimate of what will drive your organization to the outcomes wanted. Will everything you're doing achieve higher volume sales and meet the company's increased profit goals?

Maybe; maybe not. The only way you'll know is by looking at the big picture to see if it's really happening.

The best way to do that is to hold a meeting with your team to explore how your portfolio of projects, as a set, is achieving your stated objectives, as indicated by the measured performance relative to your targets. It is this step that leads us to the final step in the 4M framework: Make decisions.

## Make decisions

So far, you have your visual model, you're managing projects, and you're measuring your progress. As you go along, you're learning more about how the actions you're taking and projects you're completing drive achievement of your organization's strategy. Sometimes strategic projects don't get the results you wanted. In other instances, emerging factors in the market create new challenges that need to be addressed.

As you review your strategy in total, you and your team need to ask if what you're doing will need to be adapted to improve execution. If change is necessary, you need a way to determine what's the best way forward and what actions are required. If you don't make course corrections based on the data you gather, you may keep plodding along, seemingly making progress but not achieving your strategy goals.

One challenge embedded in the overall process is the inevitable shortfall in both data and time; you almost always wish you had better data and more time to make your choices. However, to execute effectively, you need to make decisions and move forward based on what you know at the time. In this section we give you a few tools for becoming a smarter, more confident decision maker.

### *Common decision biases*

Before you move forward any decisions, it's useful to understand the common decision traps that trip up leaders and their teams. In the HBR classic article, "Hidden Traps in Decision Making," John Hammond, Ralph Kenney, and Howard Raiffa discuss the following decision traps:

- **Anchoring:** People tending to give disproportionate weight to the first information received

- **Status quo:** The bias to perpetuate keeping things how they are

- **Sunk cost:** Allowing past investments in time or money to influence future choices when they shouldn't

- **Confirming evidence:** Seeking out information that confirms our viewpoint instead of challenging it

- **Framing:** Choosing to look at a choice in terms of the original framing of the question
- **Estimating and forecasting:** The view that estimates and forecasts are more accurate than they are[94]

You want to review these biases and keep them in mind as you go about your team's work, to adjust your execution efforts. The more impartially you can approach your decisions, the better.

### Basic decision-making process

In the Harvard Business Essentials book *Decision Making: 5 Steps to Better Results*, the authors note that sound decision making stems from having a reliable, repeatable process. Using a defined process whenever needed for a major decision will help you feel confident you're making thoughtful choices, and it will help your staff feel empowered and included. It also builds trust in your decision-making abilities.

Here is their research-backed, five-step process for decision making:

1. **Establish a context for success:** Create a safe space for brainstorming, free of bickering or infighting.
2. **Frame the issue properly:** Make sure you understand the true nature of the problem.

3. **Generate alternatives:** Good decisions can only spring from a multitude of possible choices.

4. **Evaluate the alternatives:** Assess the feasibility, risks, and implications of each option.

5. **Choose the best alternative:** Make the best decision you can, knowing you followed a thorough, methodical process.[95]

By following this step-by-step process, you can demonstrate evenhandedness, and why your chosen alternative is best. Even if a team member disagrees with your decision, they'll have confidence and respect that you followed a deliberate process.

*Course-correction meetings*

As mentioned in the previous section, it's important to periodically gauge the success of your strategy in aggregate. Because it's a hypothesis, strategy needs constant reassessment and recalibration.

Think of yourself as the captain of a competitive sailing team. Despite your preparation and planning, the race is dynamic. Winds are blowing and gusting, seas are rolling, and competitors constantly jockey for position. All of this requires constant monitoring and responding, and teams must toggle rapidly between decisions and actions. While not quite as fast paced, focused execution is otherwise similar. Without reviews and resets, teams may find themselves far behind or out of the race entirely. Course-correcting review should be frequent—say, monthly—to ensure you're staying on track.

## Course change meetings

If you've been executing your strategy and your hypothesis is proving untrue, your strategy needs to change. It's time to change your boat's direction, as Harvard professors Robert Kaplan and David Norton note in their book, *Execution Premium: Linking Strategy to Operations for Competitive Advantage*.[96]

Course changes are best when there's a major disruption to the plan. These meetings are put in place to revisit the assumptions underlying the strategy. These review meetings should stand apart from course-correction meetings and day-to-day operations issues, to ensure proper time is taken to look at the big picture. The fundamental questions here aren't about whether you are still on course, they revolve around whether you're still in the right race.

Start by discussing the highest-level strategic objective and work down from there. Is the basic strategy still sound? What about the initiatives that fulfill strategy? Maybe some are ineffective and should be replaced by new initiatives.

If you decide on a new strategy, the next step is to check your performance model still accurately reflects what the company does and how it serves customers. If not, it's time to redraw your visual map, based on your new strategy… and the focused execution cycle begins again.

What are the biggest obstacles to holding a successful strategy-review meeting? Kaplan and Norton cite lack of data, inability to test strategy, and discouraging employees from offering suggestions. Hopefully, you have your data in hand, have been road-testing your strategy, and are ready to take staff input at the meetings.

## Getting started with focused execution

In this chapter we covered the 4M execution process: Model performance, Manage projects, Measure progress, and Make decisions. The better you and your teams are at managing focused execution, the faster you'll see results.

If you're ready to hone your execution process, here are a few tips to have at the ready:

- **Set up for success.** To make the process work for you, you need to set up all the components first and then refine them over time.
- **Need for speed.** Execution is a continuous cycle. The faster you're able to move through each

element of the model, the more your execution skills will improve.

- **Time to learn.** Set aside time to learn what works and what doesn't. Adopt the best and discard the rest.

Everyone wants to execute well, but not everyone is successful. This process will put you on the fast track to results. That said, you must work the process to reap the benefits. It requires discipline and persistence, but the results are worth the effort. That's what top-tier performance is all about, which is the topic of our final chapter.

# 12
# Achieving Top-Tier Performance

Companies that thrive over the long term hail from many different industries and geographies. They all have one thing in common, though: They outperform their competitors; not by a little—by a lot. More concerning to leaders should be the related findings those in today's VUCA environment, which show that it's become increasingly difficult to reach and sustain top-tier performance. Recent McKinsey & Company research confirms this. In their database of the world's 2,000 largest companies, consultants found the top 20% of companies garnered *nearly 90%* of the total economic value created by all companies, while the bottom 20% of those companies sustained crushing economic losses.[97]

Let's look at what creates the exceptional performance that distinguishes top companies.

## Why top-tier performance?

Answering this simple question has proved quite difficult. This topic is of such interest, it has been on leaders' minds for the past forty years. It spawned one of the most widely read management books of all time: *In Search of Excellence*.[98] Authors Tom Peters and Robert Waterman, Jr, highlight eight principles of management for organizations who prefer to end up like Apple instead of Blockbuster. Since the book's first publication in 1982, new teams of researchers have launched efforts to uncover the holy grail of top-tier performance. While differences exist in each team's findings, over time, researchers are getting closer to a one-size-fits-all model, as HBR Senior Editor Julia Kirby notes in her article "Toward a Theory of High Performance."[99] As we'll see, these models can be hard to compare with each other, but some key high-impact behaviors have emerged.

If you've been reading other chapters in this book, you will have noticed that some concepts come up more than once. In this chapter you will see lots of connections with themes that we discuss elsewhere. The reason is that we've been talking all along about high-performing leaders. It should be no surprise that the best companies thrive on the things that will improve your performance as a leader. Here we bring many of those ideas together, and we also refer you to our other chapters on them.

You might be wondering why you should care about top-tier performance. Maybe this is work best left to bosses at the top. Can you really make a difference where you are? Absolutely you can. Decisions you make and actions you take impact overall company performance—sometimes dramatically. Consider the origins of one of the most successful inventions of the twentieth century.

---

**EXAMPLE: Not so strong performance**

Spencer Silver was a scientist responsible for developing stronger adhesives at 3M, the building materials and adhesives manufacturer. As part of his experimental work, he created something entirely the opposite: "Microspheres," which were sticky but removable. For years he searched for a use for the substance but couldn't find one, until another 3M scientist, Art Fry, contacted him about developing a bookmark that would stick but not damage the page it was on.

The inquiry led to one of the most widely used office inventions in modern history: The Post-it Note. Thanks to this persistence and creativity, on average every person in business now uses eleven Post-it Notes a day, and the product is sold in over 100 countries around the world.[100]

---

Post-it Notes didn't come from senior leadership—they came from Silver's extraordinary tenacity in finding a use for his discovery. The invention certainly benefited from 3M's commitment to great results, though, as seen in its organizational culture, its execution of a plan to get Post-its to market, and its clarity of focus on strategy.

In this chapter we'll share with you what is important to achieving great results. You'll discover the four proven, must-focus areas of excellence; as well as a secondary list of four additional skills, from which you need to pick at least two more. This is the *4+2 formula for success*, as the researchers that identified the practices call it. As an emerging leader, focusing on these key practices will drive your unit's success and position you as someone who understands what's required to create a top-tier organization.

## Chapter goals

The primary job of a great leader is to drive great performance. You need to provide the focus, transparency, prioritization, and shared commitment to results.

By the end of this chapter, you will be able to:

- Recognize and build top performance in your organization
- Focus your strategy and communicate it clearly

- Execute the most important activities flawlessly
- Foster a performance-oriented culture and organization structure

## What we know about top-performing organizations

How do we know which leadership skills create high-performing organizations? The insights we're drawing on come from a groundbreaking study conducted over five years, starting in 1996.[101] Further details are included in the book *What Really Works: The 4+2 Formula for Sustained Business Success*.[102] Researchers William Joyce, Nitin Nohria, and Bruce Roberson led a team that analyzed how companies used hundreds of different business tools and techniques, to discover the best predictors of long-term success. Some companies started strong but faded; others struggled initially but ultimately succeeded. A select few companies started on top and stayed there, and that's what we're all looking for. The researchers identified the top skills by examining the strengths of these consistent winners for common traits.

---

**EXERCISE: Achieving top-tier performance assessment**

How does your organization stack up? Regardless of where you work, it's never too early to think about this.

**TWELVE SKILLS**

Does your company do the things that lead to great results? While you may not know every little detail, you should have enough insight to get a sense for how well you're doing overall. That's what this assessment is designed to do.

We recommend, in instances where you might not know the answers, you spend some time seeing what you can find out. There are almost always people you can talk to in different departments who can shed light on each of the questions below. Give it a try.

Rate your organization using the following scale:
0: Never, 1: Occasionally, 2: Often, 3: Always.

Because the formula for top-tier performance comprises two different parts, the assessment is divided into two sections. Score each part separately:

| Achieving top-tier performance—self-assessment | | | | |
|---|---|---|---|---|
| Our organization creates and maintains a clearly stated, focused strategy. | 0 | 1 | 2 | 3 |
| Our teams develop and maintain flawless execution. | 0 | 1 | 2 | 3 |
| Across our organization, we develop and maintain a performance-oriented culture. | 0 | 1 | 2 | 3 |
| Our leaders have built a fast, flexible, flat organization. | 0 | 1 | 2 | 3 |
| **Primary score** | | | | |

## ACHIEVING TOP-TIER PERFORMANCE

| | | | | |
|---|---|---|---|---|
| Our organization holds onto talented employees and finds more. | 0 | 1 | 2 | 3 |
| We make industry-transforming innovations. | 0 | 1 | 2 | 3 |
| We have leaders that are committed to achieving high performance. | 0 | 1 | 2 | 3 |
| We seek growth through mergers and partnerships. | 0 | 1 | 2 | 3 |
| **Secondary score** | | | | |

If you scored greater than 10 on the first section—the "top 4" skills—your organization is on the cusp of excelling at the required capabilities of top-tier players. If not, there's an opportunity to invest time and energy in those areas essential to best-in-class organizations.

In the second section—the "+2" skills—you need to excel in two of the four areas, so don't just add up all four items. Instead, pick two capabilities that your organization focuses on, or pick two you think will have the greatest impact. Add the scores for those two together; you'll want a total score of 5 or 6.

Now add your two scores together. The closer you are to 18, the better—that's what top-tier performance looks like. If your organization is coming up short, don't fret—the rest of this chapter will discuss what high performance looks like within each practice.

## Top-tier performance defined

You might think understanding top-tier performance is easy. It's not. Some measure annual growth in revenue or income. Others evaluate performance by financial returns on assets or equity. Longevity—the duration of top-tier performance—is factored in too. Time horizons vary as well; some look at ten years, others eleven, and others twenty or more. Not so straightforward, huh? For our purposes, we'll use the same criteria as Joyce, Nohria, and Roberson:

- Top-tier performers are companies that delivered the highest total shareholder return (TSR) over the ten-year study period.
- These companies are the ones—in comparison with the others—that yielded the practices in this chapter.

## Skill builder Twelve: Four primary practices

What are the practices that lead to high performance? The four primary ones at which every organization must excel are presented in the four-practice skill builder presented below.

We put them into a sequential framework:

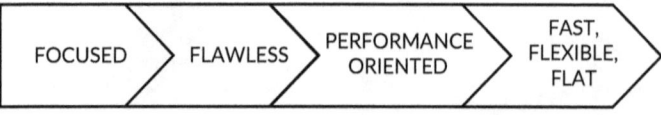

1. **Focused strategy:** Key to any winning strategy is being clear about what the strategy is and communicating it consistently to all stakeholders.

2. **Flawless execution:** Winning companies identify which processes are essential to meeting their target customers' needs, and they work to make those processes as efficient as possible—ideally doubling overall productivity at twice the industry average.

3. **Performance-oriented culture:** Winning companies design and build cultures that encourage outstanding individual and team contributions, and hold all employees responsible for success.

4. **Fast, flexible, flat organization:** Top performers implement organization structures that simplify work and streamline decision making.

These may seem simple at first glance, but you need *exceptional*, industry-leading performance to beat your competition. That's why the assessment evaluations are higher in this chapter than in others.

## Secondary practices

Before we dive deep into the four primary practices, don't forget the additional four second-tier practices, from which the +2 factors in the 4+2 formula are drawn. Companies need at least two of these to drive top-tier performance:

1. **Talent:** Top organizations that focus on this practice show a strong inclination to develop and promote their own top talent, along with their ability to retain their top performers.

2. **Innovation:** Winning companies that build innovation capabilities focus on finding new product concepts or technology breakthroughs that have the potential to disrupt their industries.

3. **Leadership:** The best organizations find top leaders—the CEO and board of directors, in particular—that are committed to the business and its employees.

4. **Mergers and partnerships:** Leading organizations that win in this practice area develop strong skills in identifying and engaging in mergers or partnerships, with organizations that augment key capabilities and that have a high likelihood of successful integration.

Over our many years consulting with leaders at both struggling and top-performing organizations, we've learned a lot about how to build excellence in the skills that generate reliable, top-tier performance. We unpack strategies and tips for you in this chapter. We'll start with how to attain excellence in each of the four main skills needed for top-tier performance.

## Focused strategy

There are huge differences between having a clear, focused strategy and having one that's mediocre. The differences are not only in the strategy itself, but in how the strategy is communicated and ultimately understood. This is so important that we wrote two whole chapters about it—don't forget to look back at Chapters 1 and 2 for more detail. Here we'll focus on five related concepts to help you develop an effective strategy.

### Build a clear value proposition

The bedrock of a great strategy is your company's value proposition—it's what you provide that appeals to those customers you target. It forms the basis of your brand promise. You need to be crystal clear regarding what your organization will be known for, both now and in the future. The three basic value propositions are based on providing one of the following:

- Excellent customer experience
- Innovative products or services
- A low-cost option

Hotel chains provide a good illustration of the different value propositions. The Ritz-Carlton provides a five-star customer experience; Yotel has created an innovative service offering; and Motel 6 delivers an operationally efficient, low-price alternative.

Value is derived from the differences across the three—differences that matter to each chain's target customers. An effective value proposition is distinctive, meaning leaders need to resist the temptation to meld all three into one. That would only confuse customers and employees.

Be sure your company's value proposition is supported by your internal process and resources. Don't make a brand promise to your customers that your team can't deliver on. If you do, your strategy and performance will sink. (For more on choosing a brand position and company strategy, flip back to Chapter 1 on strategic thinking.)

### *Take an outside-in perspective*

Henry Ford famously said, "If I'd asked customers what they wanted, they would have told me a faster horse." That way of thinking may have worked for Ford Motors at the dawn of the industrial age, but research shows it's not how winning organizations think about strategy today.

If your organization is struggling with crafting a good strategy, it's time to talk to customers. Customers will have insights on your products, services, your brand, the competition and, most importantly, the challenges they face related to the job your product or service does for them. As Clayton Christensen and his colleagues note in their article, "Know Your Customers'

'Jobs to be Done'": "The key to successful innovation is identifying the jobs that are poorly performed in customers' lives and then designing products, experiences, and processes around those jobs."[103]

Feedback that comes directly from customers often generates the best insights on strategy. For a video that explains jobs to be done, you will find a "Know Your Customers' Jobs to Be Done" clip on the Harvard Business Review website.[104]

## Sense and respond to the marketplace

Your organization's strategy doesn't exist in a vacuum. It's important to consider changes in the marketplace as they occur—before, during, and after you create and execute a strategy. Failure to do so increases the likelihood of being caught on the wrong side of a trend, potentially threatening your business in total.

Take booksellers, for example. As Amazon emerged in 1995, industry pundits predicted the downfall of small, independent booksellers. Researchers had no doubt that consumers, with millions of titles at their fingertips and algorithm-generated suggestions, would flock to the online channel; and they did. Independent booksellers did not decline, though. In fact, from 2009 to 2018, the number of independent booksellers grew 49%, according to the American Booksellers Association. By understanding Amazon's limitations and emphasizing the ways that they could create unique value, booksellers endeared themselves to both their customers and their communities. Harvard Business School professor Ryan Raffaelli highlighted the story in his working paper, "Reinventing Retail: The Novel Resurgence of Independent Bookstores."[105]

If you change how you go to market in response to an emerging trend, just be sure you can deliver the new products or services. Not all companies are able to manage the internal shift effectively. Don Sull of MIT highlights in his article "Why Good Companies Go Bad" that *active inertia* describes organizations following set patterns of behavior, even in response to dramatic changes. Following methods that have solved previous issues, market leaders simply accelerate their previous activities, which only serves to intensify the problems they are facing.[106]

### Communicate the strategy

No matter whether you work in a large organization or a startup, employees at every level make decisions every day on their own. If they don't have a firm understanding of your strategy and how they contribute to it in their specific area, the choices they make run the risk of working at odds with the strategy.

When we worked as strategy consultants, our company research found only 5% of the workforce in most organizations understands the strategy. That's a sobering statistic. How can a company execute a strategy that employees aren't even familiar with? The bottom line is it can't. To get the strategy into the hearts and hands of everyone in the organization, leaders like you need to continually revisit and reinforce what the strategy is intending to accomplish and how.

## *Tend to the core business*

Paradoxically, the pursuit of sustained growth has been the downfall of many organizations—not because growth is bad, but because companies often chase it at the expense of their core business. As they stretch for new markets, they lose focus on the things that are the foundation for their success. Profitable growth should stem from the core and leverage existing capabilities, not veer the business off course into unchartered waters. This is one of the bedrock principles discussed in *In Search of Excellence*—the book we discussed at the outset of this chapter. The authors called the principle "sticking to your knitting."[107]

This insight hasn't changed over the years. If anything, it's been reinforced. In their book *Profit from the Core: A Return to Growth in Turbulent Times,* authors Chris Zook and James Allen "found that the key to unlocking hidden sources of growth and profits is usually not to abandon the core business but to focus on it with renewed vigor and new levels of creativity."[108] Sage advice for leaders at all levels to keep in mind.

**TWELVE SKILLS**

*Get clarity on strategy first*

To summarize: Focusing your strategy is the first step toward top-tier performance. After all, if you're optimizing things that aren't central to your strategy, it won't matter how well you do them—they're unlikely to help the company grow. Once you do land on a focused strategy, the next principle is to execute expertly.

## Flawless execution

The second driver of top-tier performance comes from having excellent operational execution. For the average organization, one of the fastest routes to exceptional performance comes from improving basic operations. You will find more on this vital part of leadership in our Chapter 11.

Consider this: In 2017 researchers Raffaella Sadun, Nicholas Bloom, and John Van Reenen concluded a study of eighteen basic management practices, from 12,000 organizations across thirty-four countries. They found that fundamental operational activities (things that companies do *every day*) are still a massive challenge for many companies, but that good practices correlate strongly with business performance. They wonder then, *Why do we undervalue competent management?* We know that top-tier organizations don't fall into this trap, and now neither will you.

## Deliver products and services that meet expectations

Top performers ensure their products and services meet their customers' expectations. Interestingly, the formula for success isn't overachievement or perfection. What is required, however, is consistently providing good-quality products and services, while carefully avoiding lapses in performance. It's a simple equation but one that's a challenge to implement, especially over long periods of time.

In the fast-food space, no one outperforms Chick-fil-A when it comes to meetings customers' expectations. For the past eight years, the quick-service chain has led the industry with its eye-popping customer service score. Satisfaction surveys note that orders are consistently delivered accurately and in clean stores, which are staffed by courteous employees with a reputation for folksy greetings and willingness to help families who need an extra pair of hands. More remarkable still, the company has provided this level of service for decades—they were profiled in 2001 in an HBR article entitled "Lead for Loyalty."[109]

This kind of performance sets a high bar for any organization. The best performers rise to the challenge by focusing on processes, incorporating enabling technology, and investing in continuous improvement initiatives such as Lean and Six Sigma. As stated in one of Chick-fil-A's values, "We pursue what's next. We find energy in adapting and re-inventing how we do things from the way we work to how we care for others."[110] That's what meeting customer expectations looks like.

### *Empower the front lines to respond to customer needs*

Another key to delivering outstanding performance is enabling frontline employees to make decisions that resolve customers' challenges when and where they occur. For many organizations, this practice requires revamping policies and investing in technology and training, along with providing supervisors who can coach and mentor employees in a manner consistent with company values.

Zappos is an organization whose name has become synonymous with providing an outstanding customer experience. Despite being an online retailer, Zappos *encourages* customers to contact them via phone to discuss the concerns they have. Call center employees who engage with customers aren't evaluated using measures such as call-resolution time; on the contrary, the company celebrates employees who set record call lengths. To enable success, employees receive seven weeks of training and are encouraged to go the extra mile for customers—an apt metaphor for a shoe seller. The point here is to "Let your frontline workers be creative" in how they solve customer challenges.[111]

There's also a bonus to empowering employees in this way—they tend to like their jobs and demonstrate greater loyalty. Nobody wants to be a drone who is only allowed to execute prescribed tasks under the cautious eye of a supervisor. Empowering frontline employees is a practice that is good for customers, employees, supervisors, and organizations alike.

## *Improve productivity and eliminate waste*

In the 4+2 study, researchers found that the best companies increased productivity *twice as fast* as the average company. That's a major achievement and one that only happens when leaders prioritize productivity growth and waste reduction. If you work in a cost center, remember that you drive results too!

Consider the discount grocery chain, Aldi. Founded in 1961 in Germany by the Albrecht family, the company opened its first US store in 1976. From that one Iowa store, Aldi has grown to almost 2,300 outlets across America today. By limiting selection, pushing its private-label brands, and eliminating excess inventory and staff, the company has carved out a powerful position in the shadow of titans like Walmart. How did they do it? By focusing on supply-chain optimization while reducing all forms of waste. Each store is staffed by ten or fewer employees. The company charges for shopping bags and requires customers who use a cart to pay 25 cents to release one from their shopping cart system. This encourages patrons to return the cart so employees don't have to. The entire business is geared toward removing anything that adds inefficiencies to the system.

While you may not have the same maniacal focus on waste as the Albrechts, there's nothing stopping you from removing things that create a drag on your productivity. Can you reduce unnecessary time in meetings or eliminate lengthy emails? Can decision making be streamlined? Find and eliminate the processes and procedures that sap productivity, and you'll earn a reputation as a top-tier leader in your own right.

### Toward better operations

Your execution will improve if your organization strives to exceed customer expectations, empower employees, improve productivity, and eliminate waste. That's a huge plus for everyone who has grown weary of working amidst inefficient operations.

## Performance-oriented culture

Leaders often look at culture through different lenses. Here are two examples. Some see culture as part of the internal business environment that should be left alone, lest it be somehow tainted or disrupted. Others think of it as something to be gently nurtured, so it can serve as a warm blanket that surrounds employees while they're at work. These views—along with many others—don't consider culture as a competitive weapon. The researchers, however, discovered that when the culture is focused on high performance, it becomes a source of competitive advantage.

## *Inspire your team*

Here's a truth: Everyone likes a winner. Winning feels good. It shows employees that hard work leads to success, and people want to work somewhere that's successful. They want to feel they're part of a team that does great work, makes a difference in customers' lives, and delivers the numbers.

A leader's job is to encourage their team to strive for outstanding results, push them when they fall behind, help when necessary, and praise them when they reach their goals. That's what inspiration is; but do you inspire others?

In his article, "How to Be an Inspiring Leader," Eric Garton notes that he and his colleagues at Bain conducted a survey of 2,000 people to find out what inspired them.[112] They amassed a list of thirty-three traits, ranging from servanthood to sponsorship. Any one of those traits, if practiced, could double effectiveness in the inspiration department, but one trait emerged as being more important than any of the others: *Centeredness*. Leaders who were centered were viewed as calm under stress, empathetic with colleagues, good listeners, and present when it mattered.

It turns out that being inspirational isn't always about giving motivating speeches—more often, it's related to simply being there for your team.

### *Reward achievement*

It shouldn't come as a surprise that top-performing companies *reward* their top performers. The *What Really Works* researchers found that 90% of winning organizations tightly linked pay to performance.[113] As one of our colleagues told us early in our careers: If you want people to focus on something (like top-tier performance), pay them for it.

Interestingly, reward doesn't have to be monetary to be effective—non-monetary incentives can work just as effectively. Just keep in mind that you get what you reward. Returning to our Zappos example: If you reward employees for staying on the phone engaging with customers, they will.

### *Create the right work environment*

During the 1960s, when the US and Soviet Union were immersed in the race to put a man on the moon, a story emerged regarding President Kennedy's visit to NASA. Allegedly, he met a janitor and asked him what his job at the fledgling agency was. "To put a man on the moon," stated the worker proudly. The response may seem funny, given what we know about janitorial work. However, in a performance-oriented culture, *everyone* contributes to the ultimate success of the mission, no matter what they do.

Does your organization celebrate everyone's work, or are some parts of the organization deemed more valuable than others? Don't let that be the case on your teams. Every worker in every department should feel their inputs are vital to success.

## *Establish and live your values*

Company values matter—a lot. If you're tempted to think they don't, take a stroll down memory lane to the ethical lapses that shook the business world in the early 2000s. Enron, Sunbeam, WorldCom, and Arthur Andersen were all wiped off the business landscape because they failed to live up to values. In today's working world, employees want to be part of something that makes a meaningful and ethical contribution to the world; that's what the ESG—environmental, social and governance—movement is all about.

All of the research we have drawn from in this chapter found that good behavior promotes good business and that weak or meaningless values lead to extinction. Winning organizations establish their values and live by them. They're not just nice-to-haves—they are an essential foundation of excellent performance. The best companies make sure every employee, from the

CEO to new hires, is indoctrinated into the company values and their importance.

We can't tell you which values to have—that's upper management's job. Your values should, however, promote a culture of ethical behavior and high performance. Look again at Chick-fil-A's values.[114] While you may not agree with every one of them, there's no denying that they contribute significantly to the company's sustained performance.

### Fast, flat, flexible organization

What type of organizational structure is best? We've heard that question often in our work, and our answer never changes: *It depends*. Typically, structure follows strategy, as the saying goes. Similarly, the *What Really Works* researchers didn't discover any one ideal organizational form. Instead, they found winning organizations reduced bureaucracy and simplified work, regardless of how they were structured.[115] Nimble companies can respond quickly to market changes and stay ahead of competitors.

Let's look at how your business is structured and whether that structure is helping or hindering performance. Middle managers have a major opportunity to shine in flatter organizations, where decision making is pushed down.

There are three practices that help optimize company structure.

## *Eliminate layers and simplify structure*

Even if companies start out flat, layers often creep in as a company grows. Many managers secretly hunger for complexity, but at steelmaker Nucor, researchers learned that management layers were limited to four,[116] no matter how large the company grew: CEO, plant manager, department head, and foreman. With fewer layers of bureaucracy than its competitors, Nucor had less red tape slowing needed changes as the steel industry evolved. Its flat bureaucracy kept it a top performer.

How does limiting bureaucracy benefit organizations? First off, it streamlines decision making, since fewer departments and managers need to weigh in. Second, a reduction in oversight contributes to faster processes. Finally, with fewer managers and focused processes, responsibility is pushed closer to the frontline, empowering staff and increasing engagement. Together, these enhancements drive up productivity and performance.

Be vigilant about reviewing your company's structure and keep cutting red tape—it needs to be a continuous activity rather than a one-time initiative.

## Encourage sharing and cooperation

In large organizations, it's common for the right hand to be unaware of what the left is doing. For example, sales may not be coordinating with marketing on their mid-level campaigns. Regional actions in one part of the business may be proceeding without aligning with national initiatives. Some of the causes for lack of coordination may be structural, for example because there's no one to integrate across functions. Other challenges might be behavioral—Northeast division leaders may believe Western-states managers don't have insights that could improve their operations, so they don't bother asking. Regardless of why, these disconnects degrade performance.

The best leaders know that the real competition isn't with colleagues on the inside—it's with competitors on the outside. To combat this, you need to be a leader that punches through barriers and eliminates silos. Take the initiative to provide incentives for cooperation among units and reward collaboration, and your organization will start reaping the benefits.

## Put the right people in place

Streamlining structure and promoting coordination won't be of much value if there are significant gaps in employee capabilities. It's ultimately the leader's job to ensure right people in the right positions, and you need to be mindful of people's strengths and interests as well as their limitations. Sometimes it's better to keep a strong individual contributor in place rather than promoting them into a management role where their best skills and interests may not be aligned. You need to skillfully manage the career paths of your technical experts alongside your generalists, and those of your rising stars with your second-string players.

In flat organizations middle managers enjoy more decision-making power because, as we've noted before, decision making is pushed down through the organization. Helping your organization to staff effectively will give you a bigger role in shaping the company's future direction.

Keep in mind that not everyone wants more responsibility. As you flatten your structure, it's important that everyone, from middle management to frontline workers, fits into the right mold for them. They need to enjoy opportunities to contribute ideas, while being given the autonomy to act independently. Look at your team and think about whether each member has the mettle to drive performance, solve problems, and suggest improvements.

### Select your key secondary practices

You'll recall that the *What Really Works* research team found winners had at least two secondary initiatives where they excelled, beyond the four core areas that count towards the +2 in the framework for top-tier performance. Let's explore each of these practices to discover which two of these four would most readily apply to your company.

### *Attract and retain key talent*

As we noted above, the battle for talent is fierce. For many companies, key positions remain open due to a lack of qualified workers. How do the best organizations contend with this?

Winning organizations build strong talent pipelines, enabling them to promote from within. They accomplish this by providing top-shelf training programs to help people advance. They also design (and redesign) jobs to challenge their employees. To be successful, talent development and retention are given a personal commitment from leaders at all levels.

### *Build committed leaders*

Due to decades of layoffs, closures, and downsizing, few companies enjoy loyalty from their employees. This leads to high turnover rates and job transitions. Top-performing companies counter this trend by growing and installing leaders—especially at the top—who are centered. They are committed to the financial success of the organization, as well as people at all levels, and who make it a point to look for challenges and opportunities across the business. This kind of leader instills this behavior from top to bottom in the organization.

Your goal is to develop leaders who identify with the company's values and mission, and who stay with the company year after year. Leaders like this embody the values needed to thrive over the long term, while equipping their staff to reflect those values in their work.

## Innovate with enthusiasm

Innovation is more than simply creating new products or improving old ones. It's a culture that embraces flexibility, creativity, and continuous improvement. Sometimes innovation in marketing, supply-chain, or delivery methods can be revolutionary—think of Netflix switching to streaming instead of mailing out videos. For top performers, it doesn't matter if innovation is incremental or disruptive—whatever generates increased productivity and performance will suffice. Top-performing organizations are relentless in their pursuit of doing business better, even if it means cannibalizing their own products. They have a comprehensive approach to improving every aspect of operations, not just their end products or services. That's what separates the best performers from the also rans.

## Grow through mergers and acquisitions

One question many companies don't ask enough: Would it make more sense for us to develop a competency or create a new product or service, or would it be better to merge or partner instead?

**TWELVE SKILLS**

Today traditional boundaries between companies, competitors, and suppliers have changed. In some cases, competitors in one arena are collaborators in another—a practice that has been growing since the 1990s, note Adam Bradenburger and Barry Nalebuff in "The Rules of Co-opetition."[117] They say that, at the simplest level, it can be a way to save costs and avoid duplicating effort. In other cases, time constraints or resource limitations make it impossible to accomplish company goals in-house. That's why many top performers focus on core competencies and outsource everything else to key partners. The key to success in this area lies in building skill in partnering or merging, alongside being circumspect in how the partner organization's resources and capabilities will be leveraged with your existing business.

## Putting it all together

At this point, you know the areas of operations that winning organizations excel at: Focused strategy; flawless operations; a performance-oriented culture; and a flat, flexible, fast organization. You've also learned that your company needs to master two secondary practices from the list of four: Recruiting and retaining top talent, building committed leaders, being enthusiastic innovators, and growing through mergers and acquisitions.

Wondering how you can help your company become a true top-tier performer in these areas? It can feel overwhelming; it's not just one or two things your

## ACHIEVING TOP-TIER PERFORMANCE

organization needs to do well—it's six. Here are some tips on achieving top-tier performance you can impact:

- **Consider your industry.** Take the time to understand your industry. Find out who the top competitors are—as well as the laggards—and understand how everyone is performing. Look at key metrics such as growth, profitability, and productivity, for starters. Really dig in to understand what's causing the performance differences across companies. Analysis is always the best starting point.

- **Think *top performance*.** Just starting to think this way will get your leadership engine going. Many organizations are too bogged down with daily fire drills and growing to-do lists to even consider what top performance looks like. Socialize the 4+2 model for becoming a long-term winning organization, and get everyone thinking that success isn't serendipity—it's a formula.

- **Pick a starting point and start.** It's unlikely you can optimize six areas at once. Choose a starting point you can impact at your level and make changes to improve performance. Be sure to measure progress, then move on to other areas while maintaining the work you started. Your initial wins should help you gain support and garner more resources for tackling difficult changes.

Managers who focus on developing these practices get better results and position themselves to move up.

That means the results of your efforts to drive top-tier performance by using the 4+2 model should be clearly evident to higher-ups, demonstrating that you're a leader with vision *and* a plan to achieve it.

## Getting started with top-tier performance

The final skill covered the 4+2 model for achieving top-tier performance. Mastering this skill would be hard to do on your own. Fortunately, you don't have to. Here's what you can do:

- **Internalize the practices.** The 4+2 formula isn't complex, but it is comprehensive. Take the time to review and learn it.

- **Get support.** Share what you've learned with you colleagues, to get them thinking about top-tier performance with you. You will need their help to get there.

- **Pick one.** Select one of the primary practices as a starting point, then get going.

Achieving top-tier performance is a lofty goal, but it is one that can be achieved. The 4+2 model provides the blueprint for any organization looking to become best in class. It's well worth the time to inculcate these practices in your company. Master them, and you will find yourself in the C-Suite in no time.

# Conclusion

## Where to go next

If you've followed your own interests to learn the leadership skills that are your top priorities, you may still have a few topics to flip back to and visit now. Maybe you've focused so far on strategy and results? If so, head to the sections on talent and teams or communication and change.

If you've read through this entire book, you now understand how to master all twelve of our top leadership skills. You're ready to put the new tools and techniques you've learned into action at your organization. Remember, though, to come back every once in a while and retake the assessments in the relevant chapters, or the complete assessment highlighted at the beginning of the book. Consider where you are excelling and where you might benefit from reviewing the chapter again. Congrats!

## Your action guide for stronger leadership

If you've made it this far and learned how to master all twelve of our leadership skills, kudos to you. Now the really hard work begins. It is time to start using these tools in your workplace. Test the principles and look for feedback and results. Some things will work right away; others may require more time, effort, and support from colleagues. Either way, keep at it. Come back to this book over and over. As you advance in your work, your role as a leader will shift, and you may need a refresher.

This book is intended as a guide and a transformative action plan. We want you to start *using* what you've learned here, to become a more successful leader, and to advance in your career. Our hope is that you will try out all these techniques at your workplace.

We don't imagine you'll suddenly be a different sort of leader in a dozen ways all at once. We recommend that you choose a skill or two that offers your biggest growth opportunities. If you're not sure which skill to prioritize, consider sitting down with a group of colleagues or your supervisor to discuss.

## CONCLUSION

Where do you have the most potential to improve? Start there. As you master your top-priority leadership skills, move on to work on additional skills. For a refresher on the current state of your leadership abilities, consider taking or retaking our Twelve Skills Self-Assessment at www.surveymonkey.com/r/TwelveSkills2. Then come back and revisit a chapter or two. This is not the kind of book you read once and leave behind. You will grow as a leader and then be challenged in new ways. Periodically, you should take stock of where you can develop and revisit some of these principles.

## One step that rules them all

No matter which leadership skill you decide to focus on, or in which order you implement your new techniques, there's one essential step you must take. It's the same step, no matter which skill you're working on. Can you guess what it is? It's feedback from your key stakeholders.

For most leaders, your key stakeholders are the people who report to you, those you work with, and your supervisors. Find those trusted colleagues, coworkers, and direct reports, and ask them how you're doing. Ask them if your communication in meetings is clear. Ask them if your leadership presence is growing. Above all else, keep soliciting feedback. Have them provide an honest assessment.

As you change your leadership approach, getting repeated feedback over time is the only way you will know if your efforts are paying off. Becoming a better leader is about making a bigger impact on the people around you. You'll never know if you're making progress without asking the people you work with how you're doing, so ask.

We would of course love *your* feedback. If this book delivers excellent results, or if you have ideas on how we could make the next edition even better, we'd love to hear from you. Email us at ed@twelveskills.com or laura@twelveskills.com.

We wish you the very best on your journey forward as a leader.

# Notes

1. Harvard Business Review, *HBR Guide to Thinking Strategically* (Harvard Business Review Press, 2019), https://store.hbr.org/product/hbr-guide-to-thinking-strategically/10237, accessed February 20, 2023
2. N Bowman, 4 Ways to Improve Your Strategic Thinking Skills (*Harvard Business Review*, 2016) https://hbr.org/2016/12/4-ways-to-improve-your-strategic-thinking-skills, accessed February 20, 2023
3. L Lai, Being a Strategic Leader Is About Asking the Right Questions (*Harvard Business Review*, 2017), https://hbr.org/2017/01/being-a-strategic-leader-is-about-asking-the-right-questions, accessed February 20, 2023, Copyright © 2017 by Harvard Business Publishing, all rights reserved, reprinted by permission
4. R Hackett, *Peloton: An oral history—from "janky, broken" prototype bikes to Champagne bottle-popping* (Fortune, 2021), https://fortune.com/2021/02/04/peloton-bike-company-oral-history, accessed February 21, 2023
5. A Mak, *Peloton Is the Rise-and-Fall Story of Our Pandemic-Scarred Times* (Slate, 2022), https://slate.com/business/2022/01/peloton-stock-production-supply-chain-problems.html, accessed February 21, 2023

6. RM Kanter, Managing Yourself: Zoom In, Zoom Out (*Harvard Business Review*, 2011), https://hbr.org/2011/03 managing-yourself-zoom-in-zoom-out, accessed February 21, 2023
7. https://www.shell.com/energy-and-innovation/the-energy-future.html, accessed February 21, 2023
8. Panasonic Group, *Matsushita Announces the True Mission of the Company*, https://holdings.panasonic/global/corporate/about/history/chronicle/1932.html, accessed February 21, 2023
9. A Webb, How to Do Strategic Planning Like a Futurist (*Harvard Business Review*, 2019), https://hbr.org/2019/07 how-to-do-strategic-planning-like-a-futurist, accessed February 21, 2023, Copyright © 2019 by Harvard Business Publishing, all rights reserved, reprinted by permission
10. F Vermeulen, Many Strategies Fail Because They're Not Actually Strategies (*Harvard Business Review*, 2017), https://hbr.org/2017/11/many-strategies-fail-because-theyre-not-actually-strategies, accessed February 21, 2023
11. DJ Collis, Why Do So Many Strategies Fail? (*Harvard Business Review*, 2021), https://hbr.org/2021/07/why-do-so-many-strategies-fail, accessed February 21, 2023
12. DJ Collis and MG Rukstad, Can You Say What Your Strategy Is? (*Harvard Business Review*, 2008), https://hbr.org/2008/04/can-you-say-what-your-strategy-is, accessed February 21, 2023, Copyright © 2008 by Harvard Business Publishing, all rights reserved, reprinted by permission
13. EA Barrows and A Neely, *Managing Projects in Turbulent Times* (Harvard Business Publishing, 2012), http://34.219.95.87/pdfs/Managing%20Projects%20 in%20Turbulent%20Times%20V2%20w%20copyright.pdf, accessed February 21, 2023
14. D Lidow, A Better Way to Set Strategic Priorities (*Harvard Business Review*, 2017), https://hbr.org/2017/02/a-better-way-to-set-strategic-priorities, accessed February 21, 2023
15. D Spradlin, Are You Solving the Right Problem? (*Harvard Business Review*, 2012), https://hbr.org/2012/09/are-you-solving-the-right-problem, accessed February 21, 2023
16. T Wedell-Wedellsborg, What's Your Problem?: To Solve Your Toughest Problems, Change the Problems You Solve (*Harvard Business Review*, 2020), https://store.hbr.org/product/what-s-your-problem-to-solve-your-toughest-problems-change-the-problems-you-solve/10257, accessed February 21, 2023

# NOTES

17  T Wedell-Wedellsborg, What's Your Problem?: To Solve Your Toughest Problems, Change the Problems You Solve (*Harvard Business Review*, 2020), https://store.hbr.org/product/what-s-your-problem-to-solve-your-toughest-problems-change-the-problems-you-solve/10257, accessed February 21, 2023, Copyright © 2020 by Harvard Business Publishing, all rights reserved, reprinted by permission

18  P Bregman, Are You Trying to Solve the Wrong Problem? (*Harvard Business Review*, 2015), https://hbr.org/2015/12/are-you-solving-the-wrong-problem, accessed February 21, 2023

19  T Ohno, *Toyota Production System: Beyond Large-Scale Production* (Productivity Press, 1988)

20  E Ries, The Five Whys (*Harvard Business Review*, 2012), https://hbr.org/2012/02/the-5-whys.html, accessed February 21, 2023

21  P Cappelli, Bring Back the Organization Man (*Harvard Business Review*, 2012), https://hbr.org/2012/03/bring-back-the-organization-ma, accessed February 21, 2023

22  B George, "Episode 500: Becoming a More Authentic Leader," HBR IdeaCast (2015), https://hbr.org/podcast/2015/12/becoming-a-more-authentic-leader, accessed February 21, 2023

23  C Gerwin, "The Secrets of Her Success," *Commonwealth*, 1998, https://commonwealthmagazine.org/uncategorized/the-secrets-of-her-success, accessed February 21, 2023

24  N Merchant, *Steve Jobs's Legacy: Design Your Own Life* (*Harvard Business Review*, 2011), https://hbr.org/2011/10/steve-jobs-legacy-design-your, accessed February 21, 2023

25  D Clark, Reinventing Your Personal Brand (*Harvard Business Review*, 2011), https://hbr.org/2011/03/reinventing-your-personal-brand, accessed February 21, 2023

26  JH Zenger, J Folkman, and S Edinger, Making Yourself Indispensable (*Harvard Business Review*, 2011), https://hbr.org/2011/10/making-yourself-indispensable, accessed February 21, 2023

27  J Baldoni, Developing Your Leadership Presence (*Harvard Business Review*, 2009), https://store.hbr.org/product/developing-your-leadership-presence/H003VH, accessed February 21, 2023

28  J Beeson, Deconstructing Executive Presence (*Harvard Business Review*, 2012), https://hbr.org/2012/08/de-constructing-executive-pres, accessed February 21, 2023

29. G Ng, *The Unspoken Rules: Secrets to Starting Your Career Off Right* (Harvard Business Review Press, 2021)
30. Jay A Conger, The Necessary Art of Persuasion (*Harvard Business Review*, 1998), https://hbr.org/1998/05/the-necessary-art-of-persuasion, accessed May 5, 2023
31. Bo Groysberg and M Slind, *The Silent Killer of Big Companies* (*Harvard Business Review*, 2012), https://hbr.org/2012/10/the-silent-killer-of-big-companies, accessed February 22, 2023
32. L Landry, *8 Essential Leadership Communication Skills* (Harvard Business School, 2019), https://online.hbs.edu/blog/post/leadership-communication, accessed February 28, 2023
33. D Roebuck, *Communication Strategies for Today's Managerial Leader* (Business Expert Press, 2012), Copyright © 2012 by Business Expert Press, all rights reserved, reprinted by permission
34. D Roebuck, *Communication Strategies for Today's Managerial Leader* (Business Expert Press, 2012), Copyright © 2012 by Business Expert Press, all rights reserved, reprinted by permission
35. R Maruf, *Better.com CEO Fires 900 Employees over Zoom* (CNN Business, 2021), https://edition.cnn.com/2021/12/05/business/better-ceo-fires-employees/index.html, accessed February 22, 2023
36. L Kim, *16 Eye-Popping Statistics You Need to Know About Visual Content Marketing* (Inc., 2015), www.inc.com/larry-kim/visual-content-marketing-16-eye-popping-statistics-you-need-to-know.html, accessed February 22, 2023
37. D Barraclough, *9 People Who Were Fired for Posting on Social Media* (Expert Market, 2023), www.inc.com/larry-kim/visual-content-marketing-16-eye-popping-statistics-you-need-to-know.html, accessed February 22, 2023
38. M Tamble, *7 Tips for Using Visual Content Marketing* (SocialMediaToday, 2019), www.socialmediatoday.com/news/7-tips-for-using-visual-content-marketing/548660, accessed February 22, 2023
39. K Holmes and J Passantino, "Tucker Carlson sent a racist text to a producer: 'It's not how white men fight'." (CNN Business, 2023), http://www.cnn.com/2023/05/03/media/tucker-carlson-text-message/index.html, accessed 10 May 2023

40. B Nilsson, *Inappropriate Text Messages Are Grounds for Dismissal* (Lexology, 2019), www.lexology.com/library/detail.aspx?g=6e7fecee-9598-4bdc-a719-ef19411f7923, accessed February 22, 2023
41. J Clifton, The Power of Work Friends (*Harvard Business Review*, 2022), https://hbr.org/2021/07/why-do-so-many-strategies-fail, accessed February 22, 2023
42. Linda A Hill, *Building Effective One-On-One Work Relationships: Background* note (Harvard Business School, 1996), www.hbs.edu/faculty/Pages/item.aspx?num=16799, accessed 28 March 2023
43. Daniel Goleman, What Makes a Leader? (*Harvard Business Review*, 2004), https://hbr.org/2004/01/what-makes-a-leader, accessed February 22, 2023, Copyright © 2004 by Harvard Business Publishing, all rights reserved, reprinted by permission
44. K Rollag, Succeed in New Situations (*Harvard Business Review*, 2015), https://hbr.org/2015/12/succeed-in-new-situations, accessed February 22, 2023, Copyright © 2015 by Harvard Business Publishing, all rights reserved, reprinted by permission
45. J Dougherty, 5 Steps to Building Great Business Relationships (*Harvard Business Review*, 2014), https://hbr.org/2014/12/5-steps-to-building-great-business-relationships, accessed February 22, 2023, Copyright © 2014 by Harvard Business Publishing, all rights reserved, reprinted by permission
46. Z Ivcevic, R Stern, and A Faas, Research: What Do People Need to Perform at a High Level? (*Harvard Business Review*, 2021), https://hbr.org/2021/05/research-what-do-people-need-to-perform-at-a-high-level, accessed February 22, 2023
47. P Cappelli, Talent Management for the Twenty-First Century (*Harvard Business Review*, 2008), https://hbr.org/2008/03/talent-management-for-the-twenty-first-century, accessed February 22, 2023
48. HBS Press, Hiring Process: Attracting the Best People (*Harvard Business School Press*, 2002), https://hbsp.harvard.edu/product/7027BC-PDF-ENG, accessed February 21, 2023, Copyright © 2022 by Harvard Business Publishing, all rights reserved, reprinted by permission

**TWELVE SKILLS**

49  MD Watkins, *7 Ways to Set Up a New Hire for Success* (*Harvard Business Review*, 2019), https://hbr.org/2019/05/7-ways-to-set-up-a-new-hire-for-success, accessed February 22, 2023

50  Adapted from J Zenger and J Folkman, Your Employees Want the Negative Feedback You Hate to Give (*Harvard Business Review*, 2014), https://hbr.org/2014/01/your-employees-want-the-negative-feedback-you-hate-to-give, accessed February 22, 2023, Copyright © 2014 by Harvard Business Publishing, all rights reserved, reprinted by permission

51  Leading Effectively staff, *Use Situation-Behavior-Impact (SBI)™ to Understand Intent* (Center for Creative Leadership, 2020), www.ccl.org/articles/leading-effectively-articles/closing-the-gap-between-intent-vs-impact-sbii, accessed February 23, 2023

52  L Pearson and N Numfor, "Leader as Coach and Mentor" (Harvard Business Publishing Education, 2021), https://hbsp.harvard.edu/product/BEP579-PDF-ENG, accessed February 23, 2023, Copyright © 2021 by Harvard Business Publishing, all rights reserved, reprinted by permission

53  Peter Cappelli and Anna Tavis, The Performance Management Revolution (*Harvard Business Review*, 2016), https://hbr.org/2016/10/the-performance-management-revolution, accessed February 23, 2016

54  YV Durme and N Vandaele, *Human Capital Trends 2019— Leading the social enterprise: Reinvent with human focus* (Deloitte, 2019), www2.deloitte.com/be/en/pages/human-capital/articles/human-capital-trends-2019.html, accessed February 23, 2023

55  A Edmondson, *The Importance of Teaming* (Harvard Business School, 2012), https://hbswk.hbs.edu/item/the-importance-of-teaming, accessed February 27, 2023

56  JR Katzenbach and DK Smith, The Discipline of Teams (*Harvard Business Review*, 1993), https://hbr.org/1993/03/the-discipline-of-teams-2, accessed February 23, 2023, Copyright © 1993 by Harvard Business Publishing, all rights reserved, reprinted by permission

57  R Lueke, Creating Teams with an Edge (*Harvard Business Essentials*) (Harvard Business Review Press, 2004), Copyright © 2004 by Harvard Business Publishing, all rights reserved, reprinted by permission

# NOTES

58  E Bernstein, *Leadership and Teaming* (Harvard Business School, 2015), www.hbs.edu/faculty/Pages/item.aspx?num=45550, accessed February 23, 2023

59  BW Tuckman, "Developmental sequence in small groups," *Psychological Bulletin*, 63(6) (1965), 384–399. https://doi.org/10.1037/h0022100

60  JR Katzenbach and DK Smith, The Discipline of Teams (*Harvard Business Review*, 1993), https://hbr.org/1993/03/the-discipline-of-teams-2, accessed February 23, 2023, Copyright © 1993 by Harvard Business Publishing, all rights reserved, reprinted by permission

61  FutureThink, *Project Aristotle and High Performing Teams* (FutureThink, 2016), www.futurethink.com.sg/project-aristotle-2/#:~:text=Psychological%20Safety,psychological%20safety%E2%80%9D, accessed March 30, 2023

62  K Behfar and R Goldberg, *Conflict Management in Teams* (Darden School of Business, 2015), https://store.hbr.org/product/conflict-management-in-teams/UV6944, accessed February 23, 2023

63  A Jay, How To Run a Meeting (*Harvard Business Review*, 1976), https://hbr.org/1976/03/how-to-run-a-meeting, accessed February 23, 2023, Copyright © 1976 by Harvard Business Publishing, all rights reserved, reprinted by permission

64  K Behfar and R Goldberg, *Conflict Management in Teams* (Darden School of Business, 2015), https://store.hbr.org/product/conflict-management-in-teams/UV6944, accessed February 23, 2023

65  E Bernstein, *Leadership and Teaming* (Harvard Business School, 2015), www.hbs.edu/faculty/Pages/item.aspx?num=45550, accessed February 23, 2023

66  R Cross, Where We Go Wrong with Collaboration (*Harvard Business Review*, 2022), https://hbr.org/2022/04/where-we-go-wrong-with-collaboration, accessed February 23, 2023

67  J Moss, *The Pandemic Changed Us. Now Companies Have to Change Too.* (*Harvard Business Review*, 2022), https://hbr.org/2022/07/the-pandemic-changed-us-now-companies-have-to-change-too, accessed February 23, 2023

68  H Ibarra and MT Hansen, Are You a Collaborative Leader? (*Harvard Business Review*, 2011), https://hbr.org/2011/07/are-you-a-collaborative-leader, accessed February 23, 2023

**TWELVE SKILLS**

69  DE Sanger, JE Barnes, and K Conger, "As Tanks Rolled Into Ukraine, So Did Malware. Then Microsoft Entered the War," *The New York Times* (February 28, 2022), www.nytimes.com/2022/02/28/us/politics/ukraine-russia-microsoft.html, accessed February 23, 2023

70  J Abele, Bringing Minds Together (*Harvard Business Review*, 2011), https://hbr.org/2011/07/bringing-minds-together, accessed February 23, 2023

71  P Adler, C Heckscher, and L Prusak, Building a Collaborative Enterprise (*Harvard Business Review*, 2011), https://hbr.org/2011/07/building-a-collaborative-enterprise, accessed February 23, 2023

72  HK Gardner and I Matviak, Performance Management Shouldn't Kill Collaboration (*Harvard Business Review*, 2022), https://hbr.org/2022/09/performance-management-shouldnt-kill-collaboration, accessed February 23, 2023

73  N Bennett and GJ Lemoine, What VUCA Really Means for You (*Harvard Business Review*, 2014), https://hbr.org/2014/01/what-vuca-really-means-for-you, accessed February 23, 2023

74  M Galbraith, Don't Just Tell Employees Organizational Changes Are Coming — Explain Why (*Harvard Business Review*, 2018), https://hbr.org/2018/10/dont-just-tell-employees-organizational-changes-are-coming-explain-why, accessed February 23, 2023

75  D Lancefield and C Rangen, 4 Actions Transformational Leaders Take (*Harvard Business Review*, 2021), https://hbr.org/2021/05/4-actions-transformational-leaders-take, accessed February 23, 2023

76  D Lancefield and C Rangen, "4 Actions Transformational Leaders Take," Copyright © 2021 by Harvard Business Publishing, all rights reserved, reprinted by permission

77  R Raffaelli, *Leading and Managing Change* (Harvard Business School, 2014), www.hbs.edu/faculty/Pages/item.aspx?num=48209, accessed February 23, 2023

78  R Kegan and L Lahey, The Real Reason People Won't Change (*Harvard Business Review*, 2021), https://hbr.org/2001/11/the-real-reason-people-wont-change, accessed February 23, 2023

79  R Kegan and L Lahey, *The Real Reason People Won't Change*, Copyright © 2021 by Harvard Business Publishing, all rights reserved, reprinted by permission

80 Harvard Business Press, *Managing Change: Expert Solutions to Everyday Challenges* (Harvard Business Press, 2009), https://store.hbr.org/product/managing-change/13279, accessed February 23, 2023, Copyright © 2009 by Harvard Business Publishing, all rights reserved, permission pending

81 MA Roberto and AC Edmondson, "Leadership and Team Simulation: Everest V3" (Harvard Business Publishing, 2017), https://hbsp.harvard.edu/product/8867-HTM-ENG?Ntt=mount%20everest, accessed February 23, 2023

82 KK Reardon, Office Politics Isn't Something You Can Sit Out (*Harvard Business Review*, 2015), https://hbr.org/2008/04/can-you-say-what-your-strategy-is, accessed February 27, 2023, Copyright © 2015 by Harvard Business Publishing, all rights reserved, permission pending

83 C Gallow, The Art of Persuasion Hasn't Changed in 2,000 Years (*Harvard Business Review*, 2021), https://hbr.org/2019/07/the-art-of-persuasion-hasnt-changed-in-2000-years, accessed February 27, 2023

84 R Cialdini, The Uses (and Abuses) of Influence (*Harvard Business Review*, 2013), https://hbr.org/2013/07/the-uses-and-abuses-of-influence, accessed February 27, 2023

85 S Covey, *The 7 Habits Of Highly Effective People* (Simon & Schuster, 1989)

86 G McKeown, Stephen R. Covey Taught Me Not to Be Like Him (*Harvard Business Review*, 2012), https://hbr.org/2012/07/stephen-r-covey-taught-me-not, accessed February 27, 2023

87 D Ulrich, J Zenger, and N Smallwood, *Results-Based Leadership: How Leaders Build the Business and Improve the Bottom Line* (Harvard Business Review Press, 1999)

88 P Leinwand and J Rotering, How to Excel at Both Strategy and Execution (*Harvard Business Review*, 2017), https://hbr.org/2017/11/how-to-excel-at-both-strategy-and-execution, accessed February 27, 2023

89 C Cote, *5 Keys to Successful Strategy Execution* (Harvard Business School, 2020), https://online.hbs.edu/blog/post/strategy-execution, accessed February 27, 2023

90 C Zook and J Allen, *Profit from the Core: A Return to Growth in Turbulent Times* (Harvard Business Publishing, 2010)

91. M Porter, What is Strategy? (*Harvard Business Review*, 2021), https://hbr.org/1996/11/what-is-strategy, accessed February 27, 2023
92. RS Kaplan and DP Norton, Having Trouble with Your Strategy? Then Map It (*Harvard Business Review*, 2000), https://hbr.org/2000/09/having-trouble-with-your-strategy-then-map-it, accessed February 27, 2023
93. A Osterwalder, A Better Way to Think About Your Business Model (*Harvard Business Review*, 2013), https://hbr.org/2013/05/a-better-way-to-think-about-yo, accessed February 27, 2023, Copyright © 2013 by Harvard Business Publishing, all rights reserved, reprinted by permission
94. JS Hammond, RL Keeney, and H Raiffa, The Hidden Traps in Decision Making (*Harvard Business Review*, 1998), https://hbr.org/1998/09/the-hidden-traps-in-decision-making-2, accessed February 28, 2023, all rights reserved, reprinted with permission
95. *Harvard Business Review, Harvard Business Essentials: Decision Making: 5 Steps to Better Results* (Harvard Business Review Review Press, 2006)
96. RS Kaplan and DP Norton, *Execution Premium: Linking Strategy to Operations for Competitive Advantage* (Harvard Business Review Press, 2008)
97. C Bradley, M Hirt, and S Smit, *Strategy To Beat the Odds* (*McKinsey Quarterly*, 2018), www.mckinsey.com/capabilities/strategy-and-corporate-finance/our-insights/strategy-to-beat-the-odds, accessed February 27, 2023
98. TJ Peters and RH Waterman, Jr, *In Search of Excellence: Lessons from America's Best-Run Companies* (Harper Business, 2006)
99. J Kirby, Toward a Theory of High Performance (*Harvard Business Review*, 2005), https://hbr.org/2005/07/toward-a-theory-of-high-performance, accessed February 28, 2023
100. *History Timeline: Post-it® Notes*, www.post-it.com/3M/en_US/post-it/contact-us/about-us, accessed February 28, 2023
101. N Nohria, W Joyce, and B Roberson, What Really Works (*Harvard Business Review*, 2003), accessed February 28, 2023
102. W Joyce, N Nohria, and B Roberson, *What Really Works: The 4+2 Formula For Sustained Business Success* (Harper Business, 2004)
103. CM Christensen, T Hall, K Dillon, and DS Duncan, Know Your Customers' "Jobs to Be Done" (*Harvard Business

## NOTES

      *Review*, 2016), https://hbr.org/2016/09/know-your-customers-jobs-to-be-done, accessed February 28, 2023
104  "Know Your Customers' Jobs to Be Done" (*Harvard Business Review*, 2018), https://hbr.org/video/5852531897001/know-your-customers-jobs-to-be-done, accessed February 28, 2023
105  RL Raffaelli, *Reinventing Retail: The Novel Resurgence of Independent Bookstores* (Harvard Business School, 2020), www.hbs.edu/ris/Publication%20Files/20-068_c19963e7-506c-479a-beb4-bb339cd293ee.pdf, accessed February 28, 2023
106  D Sull, Why Good Companies Go Bad (*Harvard Business Review*, 1999), https://hbr.org/1999/07/why-good-companies-go-bad, accessed February 28, 2023
107  TJ Peters and RH Waterman, Jr, *In Search of Excellence: Lessons from America's Best-Run Companies* (Harper Business, 2006)
108  C Zook and J Allen, *Profit from the Core: A Return to Growth in Turbulent Times* (Harvard Business Review Press, 2010)
109  FF Reichheld, Lead for Loyalty (*Harvard Business Review*, 2001), https://hbr.org/2001/07/lead-for-loyalty, accessed February 28, 2023
110  Chick-fil-A, www.chick-fil-a.com/careers/culture, accessed February 28, 2023
111  D Burkus, Let Your Frontline Workers Be Creative (*Harvard Business Review*, 2015), https://hbr.org/2015/12/let-your-frontline-workers-be-creative, accessed February 28, 2023
112  E Garton, How to Be an Inspiring Leader (*Harvard Business Review*, 2017), https://hbr.org/2017/04/how-to-be-an-inspiring-leader, accessed February 28, 2023
113  W Joyce, N Nohria, and B Roberson, *What Really Works: The 4+2 Formula For Sustained Business Success* (Harper Business, 2004)
114  Chick-fil-A, www.chick-fil-a.com/careers/culture, accessed February 28, 2023
115  W Joyce, N Nohria, and B Roberson, *What Really Works: The 4+2 Formula For Sustained Business Success* (Harper Business, 2004)
116  W Joyce, N Nohria, and B Roberson, *What Really Works: The 4+2 Formula For Sustained Business Success*
117  A Brandenburger and B Nalebuff, The Rules of Co-opetition (*Harvard Business Review*, 2021), https://hbr.org/2021/01/the-rules-of-co-opetition, accessed February 28, 2023

# Acknowledgments

This book and the work that went into it would not have been possible without the support, guidance and grace offered by so many over the years.

**Our clients.** Thanks to our clients who have taught us about real leadership—the part you can't learn at school. Leaders at large, small, government, not-for-profit, and for-profit organizations. Leaders at the top of their organizations and those just beginning their rise. We admire the difference you make every day for your companies and the people you lead.

**Our students.** We appreciate the students (and staff) at Harvard Extension School, who have shared with us and each other the joy and inspiration of lifelong learning.

**Our coworkers.** We value the work we have done together to strengthen leadership and business performance across the world. Colleagues and clients at Duke Corporate Education not only champion our work but teach us so much about leader development. The team at Core Leadership Institute taught us what following your purpose and passion actually looks like. Our Balanced Scorecard brethren from Renaissance, Balanced Scorecard Collaborative, Palladium, Ascendant, and beyond each took a simple idea and changed the world with it.

**Our book collaborators.** We could not have done it without you. Thank you. Carol Tice for holding us to a schedule, asking the right questions, and keeping ideas readable. Terry Pappy for years of support, personally and graphically. Fritz Gugelmann and Anne Helmstetter for their insightful comments and meaningful edits on the manuscript.

**Our families.** Thank you for your support, your love, and your enduring patience while we traveled during the week and worked on weekends. You make everything worthwhile.

**Our co-author.** Good partners are hard to find. Finding someone who makes you better by incorporating learning, faith, and family into every meaningful project is rare. May many more joint efforts follow this one.

# The Authors

**Ed Barrows** has over twenty-five years of hands-on experience helping corporate and government executives become better strategic leaders. His professional services experience includes Deloitte, General Electric, PwC, Palladium Group, and Duke Corporate Education. He is currently President of CLIR Coaching.

Academically, Ed has served on the faculties of Boston College and Babson College, and he currently teaches at Harvard's Division of Continuing Education. His first book with Andy Neely of Cambridge University, *Managing Performance in Turbulent Times: Analytics and*

*Insight*, was released in 2011. Ed holds a BS in Business Administration from Boston University, an MBA from Georgetown University, and a DBA from Cranfield School of Management. He also has a certificate in Evidence-Based Coaching from Fielding Graduate University.

Ed is a retired Marine Corps Lieutenant Colonel, who served in Operations Desert Storm and Iraqi Freedom. He currently lives in Greater Boston, with his wife and trying to keep up with his six children.

**Laura M Downing** has over thirty years of experience working with senior executives from for-profit and not-for-profit organizations; as well as government agencies as they strive to execute their strategy, strengthen their leadership teams, and maximize their own impact as leaders. Currently a management consultant and leadership coach, Laura is founder and CEO of CLIR Coaching—a woman-owned firm dedicated to creating leaders at all levels. Prior to this, she founded and led several professional services firms, including Balanced Scorecard Collaborative, Palladium, and Ascendant.

Laura teaches strategy, performance management, and business problem solving to a range of corporate

**THE AUTHORS**

leaders. She is also an instructor at Harvard's Division of Continuing Education, where she teaches in power and influence, and business fundamentals.

Laura holds a BS in Business Administration from Georgetown University, an MBA from Harvard School of Business Administration, and a certificate in Evidence-Based Coaching from Fielding Graduate University.

Laura lives in Boston with her husband, son, and two cats.

- www.TwelveSkills.com

- YouTube: http://www.youtube.com/@TwelveSkills-Resource

- www.linkedin.com/groups/12826353/

- https://twitter.com/MyTwelveSkills

www.ingramcontent.com/pod-product-compliance
Lightning Source LLC
Chambersburg PA
CBHW050851160426
43194CB00011B/2111